CARING ABOUT
CRYSTAL

KRISTIN B♥WEN

SYNERGY
PUBLISHING GROUP

BELMONT, NORTH CAROLINA

Caring About Crystal

Kristin Bowen

Published by Synergy Publishing Group, Belmont, NC
Layout and design by Melisa Graham

Softcover, June 2025, ISBN 978-1-960892-42-3
E-book, June 2025, ISBN 978-1-960892-43-0

Dedication

For my mother, for shaping me, even in
the ways you never intended.
For my dad, through love and pain, I found my strength.
For my daughters, you are the reason I chose to heal.
This book is proof that I survived.

CONTENTS

To my friends, family, and supporters, if you don't recognize me here, it's because I didn't even know who I was back then either. It feels like I've lived lifetimes since these journal entries, and I can only pray these words provide the hope that someone needs to make it through to the other side. What exactly is the other side, and what's over there? Well, that may be different for each of us, and I hope you can discover it for yourself through these pages.

Disclaimer: The following stories and accounts are written solely from the author's point of view and experience. Some names, dates, and places have been changed to protect others.

PART 1: FOUNDATION

THE BEGINNING

13 YEARS OLD

February 17, 1998

I can't believe she caught me. She NEVER comes home this early! I thought I had it perfectly timed but of course she came in early. I was hanging out with the neighborhood boys out at the creek and rollerblading around the neighborhood. I just got new skates for Christmas and it was nice to finally break them in. The boys always try to get me to play basketball with them but I suck so I've been working on tricks with the skates instead. I think Tommy is really cute but he doesn't seem interested in me at all. Mike is funny but also kind of a jerk. His way of flirting is making stupid jokes and teasing me about my hair. It's kind of annoying. Anyway, the boys had gotten their hands on a pack of cigarettes and after trying them, they gave me a few to keep. I dont even know why. They tasted horrible and the smoke bothered me. I was going to put them in the cellar so my mom wouldn't find them but we were still playing outside and I knew I had plenty of time. I put them on the front step and wouldn't you believe she came home EARLY. You should have seen my face when she was walking to the front door. It was like you see in the movies, where the main character is in slow motion and every second feels like an eternity. I beelined to the door, arms stretched out in front of me, sprinting as fast as I could, yelling, "nooooooooooo." Ugh, she was so pissed. I prolly shocked her. She would never think I would try something like this. It was just last year I was hiding and breaking my dads cigarettes when he would leave them around the house. I thought smoking was so gross. Pretty sure I'm grounded for a month now. Guess you'll be hearing a lot more from me for the next few weeks.

February 19, 1998

Why is my mom even surprised at any of this? She has been ushering men in and out of my life for my WHOLE life. These guys don't even care about me or about her! She throws her hands up and acts like she can't discipline me herself so they step in to try to play dad. Get out of here! They don't even know what they're doing. I picture the Charlie Brown voice in my head while they are talking, "womp, womp, womp, womp, waaaa." One time she sat me down to tell me how she was going to have Kyle start giving me consequences for my behavior so that she and I could "improve our relationship." Ha! How is that going? Are we closer now? No! Now I just resent her for the fact that she can't do it herself.

Then there's my dad. Where the hell is he all the time? Does he even care? I'm supposed to see him every other weekend and that rarely happens. I can't remember the last time he called me during the week to see how I was doing. My mom probably wouldn't let him talk to me anyway. She clearly doesn't like him. He used to live not too far from us in Philly but now he is all the way in D.C. I have to take the train to Union Station by myself which is a little terrifying. I sit there for two hours, nervous I'm going to miss my stop. The train is usually empty but one time this guy sat next to me and put this hand on my leg and started to move it up my skirt. I literally jumped up, ran to the snack cart, and hid in the bathroom until we arrived at my stop. There are weirdos on that thing. Then, one time, I got to Union Station and my dad didn't show up for what felt like two hours. I sat there in the station with my bag of clothes and no way to contact him. I didn't know if I should call the police or get a train security guard. I would have called him a million times if I had a bunch of change but I only had one quarter and I just happened to have that leftover from the money I had to buy snacks on the way there. I was worried that if I got his voicemail before I hung up then I had no way to call back and try again. After a while I did try him a couple of times but of course no answer. I don't even remember if he apologized when he finally arrived. Afterwards, he took me shopping and I got a bunch of nice new clothes and jewelry. I remember this soft plush blazer that he got me and a white button up shirt. It wasn't really my style but I knew it was expensive and he thought it looked good on me so we got it. Once I finally see him, we always have the best time laughing and being silly. It's like an escape from my regular life. Plus, I never have to do any chores since I'm just there for the weekend.

February 21, 1998

Just you and me. I've been lying on my bed daydreaming, wondering what other people's lives are like. I like it when it's quiet—just laying here. But then I have this little panic or jump inside my chest. I think I forgot something or I'm supposed to be doing something else. I close my eyes and try to just breathe and stay calm. That's the only thing I like about the night time—you're supposed to actually sleep and rest. It's the one time I don't feel bad for doing nothing.

February 22, 1998

The boys were throwing rocks at my bedroom window
yesterday to see if I could talk. I still can't leave the house
but my mom wasn't home so I hung out the window and we
played catch for a little bit. I feel like Rapunzel locked up in
her castle. Counting down the weeks til I'm out...

February 26, 1998

I feel like I'm suffocating. I'm not trying to be sassy
or mischievous. I guess you could say I am pushing the
boundaries but it's nothing against my mom. Her boyfriends,
on the other hand, are pissing me off. Stop trying to
discipline me. This guy Kyle isnt so bad. I think he actually
cares but he is such a hard ass. He will probably be gone
next month so there is no sense in me trying to get to know
him. All of the other ones were literal monsters. They make
this guy seem like an angel. Maybe I should start being a
little better. I don't want to be bad, I just feel angry all the
time. I just wish I had one person who understood me or all
that I've been going through.

March 3, 1998

I just got the whole Green Day album on tape. I'm pretty sure I've memorized every word at this point. I've been laying on my bed replaying each song and reading the lyrics until I have them stuck in my head. The lyrics are pretty ridiculous but it's so fun to sing. How can you not want to jump on your bed, screaming at the top of your lungs when DOOKIE is playing lol..."Basket Case" might be the story of my life lol.

Between Green Day and The Beastie Boys, I'm not sure which one my mom hates more. I think the minute you become a parent you begin to hate music like this because you know it's just kids acting like idiots complaining about life and their parents and how everything is hard. Maybe once you're an adult you just accept that life sucks. Ha! That sounds horrible. Well I'm gonna take this moment to forget it all and mess up my bed. Shhhh dont tell my mom.

March 4, 1998

Sometimes I wonder if everyone feels this way. Does life actually get better? Do people really like it? I just feel like everybody can't be as unhappy as I feel. I'm making a pact right now that when I get a job, it has to be something I love. There is no sense in going to work, a place you have to be allllll day, and hating it. Maybe that's the first step to happiness!

PIVOTAL MOMENTS

March 11, 1998

My moms stupid boyfriend made me write 100 sentences today because I forgot to turn off the kitchen light. 100 sentences?! That's crazy. How is that going to help me remember to turn the light off? Is it really that big of a deal? It was an accident. It seems like overkill to me. He isn't even my dad and I never asked for him to be in my life. You would think after I popped all those pills a few months ago, somebody would have taken a bit more notice about what the hell is going on with me. I mean, I wasn't trying to "get attention" like people always say. I DID want to die but then I got scared. Thank God Layla called poison control then 9-1-1. The absolute worst part was my grandma walking up as they were taking me out of the house on a stretcher and into the ambulance. Her face looked devastated like all of the blood drained from her head. After drinking that charcoal in the hospital I never want to do it again but damn, nothing even changed. We barely talked about it and surely nobody understands why I did it, not even me. After a few counseling sessions and people asking if I was ok, everything went back to "normal".

My dad hardly sees me, my mom doesn't have time to get to know the real me or my feelings and this *boyfriend* of hers is over here trying to raise me. It doesn't seem like anybody really cares about my happiness or what I want in life. Why am I so unhappy? I don't know why but what I do know is that four weeks of grounding for the little smoking incident is not helping.

Goodnight diary. Thanks for listening to me.

March 18, 1998

Well we went to see a psychiatrist. I guess the hospital referred us there. They gave me these pills that I take once a day to help with my anger or sadness or whatever the hell it is. Anyway, my mom and I call them happy pills. I feel a little blank or empty when I take them but it does take away the mean and angry feelings. I guess I would rather feel nothing than whatever the hell I was feeling before. Hope this works! Wish me luck...Sorry I haven't been writing as much. I'm finally off punishment and have been hanging outside with the boys. Talk soon!

April 2, 1998

My mom and her stupid boyfriend were fighting again. All they do is yell and argue. I don't ever see them happy together. I just don't get it. Is this what every family is like? People just go to work, come home, eat dinner and argue? If that's it, I don't want it. I guess it's better than the last boyfriend my mom had. They argued so much and I would just lock myself in my bedroom. One day it was so crazy that they were basically chasing each other around the house, trying to agitate each other. I came out of my room to find my mom hiding the knife block in the bathtub. I have no idea if she was hiding the knives from him so he wouldn't use them on her or if she put them in there to use later for self defense. This guy isn't violent like that but he still makes me do the stupidest stuff. This time I had to write 300 sentences about turning off the lights. Well, jokes on him, I still forget to turn the lights out. It just seems ridiculous. Pretty sure anything I do will never be enough for them. I don't even think I'm a bad kid but it feels like any little mistake and I'm hung out to dry.

May 3, 1998

Fuck it. My mom never believes me. I know I haven't been the best behaved recently but the fact that she can look me dead in my eyes and say I'm lying pisses me off. Now I wish we DID sneak out of that room. This whole Boston field trip has been a mess! It was supposed to be a really fun end of year trip for the entire 8th grade. Actually, it was really fun to start off with. They had all of us take a bus, not a school bus but a nice, big bus, up to Massachusetts. We were literally crawling under the seats, sliding along the ground and playing hide and seek on the bus. It was so fun. The teachers didn't even seem to care that we were acting silly. It definitely made the hours go by faster. I don't know how we got to pick our room assignments but Dana, Layla, Suzanne and I were all rooming together. We were hyped! The teachers had already scared us to death to make sure we did not leave our hotel rooms. They threatened serious consequences and we wanted no part of that. Plus, all of us were in the same room. There wasn't any reason to go poking around and see other people. We actually spent the night jumping on the hotel beds and climbing on top of the closet shelf, doing face masks and laughing hysterically. We kept hearing other kids running up and down the hallway and banging on doors. We tried to look through the little peephole to see who it was but it was too hard to tell. We knew we better not open our door or it was going to look like we snuck out too. Now, one thing that did go wrong was at one point Dana pulled out the Bible and decided to burn the edges of some of the pages. We screamed at her to stop and told her to quit being ridiculous. None of us were really religious but that just seemed dangerous and stupid. The next day was fun too. We saw all the historic stuff we were learning in class, ate out at some restaurant and got home on Sunday. Once we got back to Delaware, we were all asked to step to the side of the bus and wait for our parents. Nobody could leave until all of our parents got there. We must have looked confused. All of the other kids were grabbing their stuff and heading home. Then they told our families we left our hotel room the night before and were in big trouble including the possibility of not graduating or attending the 8th grade formal dance! Are you kidding me? We didn't leave that room! We were shocked! Nobody left that room. We all adamantly told the story of that night to our parents but nobody wanted to hear it. My mom made me write a damn letter apologizing to the administrators and teachers. For what? I don't know because I was in that room all night. No matter what I said to her or the administration, nobody listened to us. I haven't talked to my mom in days. I refuse. Only when I have to, I'll answer her questions but if she isn't going to believe me then why should I even tell her anything? I'm over it.

May 27, 1998

I don't know how to feel right now. I LOVED my hair when I first cut it but now I'm feeling really self conscious. Two days ago I had long brown hair and now it's "boy" short and practically bright orange. I went to my dad's in DC for my birthday and he knows this really fancy hairdresser. I'm pretty sure it cost like $300 just to chop and dye my hair. I was nervous but I freakin loved it. I remember walking out of there like I owned the place ya know? But then I got home and of course my mom didn't like it. She doesnt like anything my dad likes and now I'm in DELA-WHERE? So people are just going to look at me crazy. This kind of style works in the city but not here. Now I just want to hide in a hole. I'm hoping Suzanne will cut school with me tomorrow and we can just walk back to her house. I really don't wanna show my face.

MY BIRTHDAY!!!

May 29, 1998

My mom is ALWAYS blaming Suzanne for everything. Its like she thinks I'm her little pet doing and saying whatever Suzanne wants me to do. Did she ever stop and think that maybe I am the bad influence? Suzanne definitely has the look of a trouble maker with her dark eyeliner and lipstick, baggy jeans and skater gear but Suzanne never tries to peer pressure me into anything. Ok, maybe she is a little reckless but never dangerous. Anyway, we skipped first period today. I stopped at Suzanne's on the way to school and we just waited until after the bell rang. I did not want everyone staring at me. It wasn't as bad as I thought but the boys were still laughing. In my mind, I know I just need to wear it like I own it and not care what everyone else thinks but I really dont want everyone staring at me.

14 YEARS OLD

June 2, 1998

I don't know what got into me today. I brought some of the pain pills to school and took like 10 of them in the bathroom. I told my friend Layla again and of course she told the teacher. My mom picked me up from school right away and we went to the hospital. They didn't have to pump my stomach but I had to drink the damn charcoal again. I think they do that just to make you gag and throw up. My mom didn't even really say anything afterward. I don't know what she could say but I thought she would ask me questions or something. I'm glad she didn't. I don't even know what I would tell her. The happy pills were working but now they aren't. I don't really feel anything and when I DO feel something, I don't want to feel anything anymore. I dont know, I guess the pain pills are like a crutch. Funny how they call them pain pills when it actually seems to take the pain away. Maybe they should call them "no pain" pills.

June 25, 1998

I can't believe it! My mom let me go live with my dad for the summer. I guess she felt like she didn't have a choice. Honestly, I probably would have tried to run away again if she didn't let me go. Besides, what would she do with me all summer? She has to work so I would have been running around the neighborhood starting fires again haha! Like that time when the boys lit a fire in the empty milk gallon and then it got stuck to Mike's leg. That was scary but we all laugh about it now! A bunch of pyros...I mean, what kid doesn't like fire?

Anyway, it feels like a fresh start. Finally somebody listened to me. Or maybe she just doesnt want to deal with my shit anymore. I don't even care. I'm glad to get away from everything and I'll finally get to hang out with my dad.

June 26, 1998

Do you think my mom is devastated or relieved that I'm leaving? If I didn't go, I was planning to find a job and an apartment and move out on my own. I know that sounds ridiculous but I just couldn't stay there any longer.

Granted, I've been acting like a little terror for months now—sneaking out, kissing boys and smoking cigarettes. That one time she caught me trying to run away and

I had the little booklet of apartments with my notes brainstorming how to make money and live on my own. It seems crazy but I'm pretty sure I could do it. I am 14 now and pretty sure I could rake leaves and shovel snow to get some cash. If I had to, I could sleep in those abandoned houses or a shelter down the street and just save up. Well, I don't have to do that anymore! Only a couple more days til I go to my dad's and can be free!

July 2, 1998

I've been thinking about why I wanted to move in with my dad so badly. Of course I want to spend time with him more but really I just think I'll feel more safe and at peace. I never knew what to expect with my mom or the men we lived with. I still have flashbacks to this time with her boyfriend from when I was really little, like 6 or 7 years old. I guess he cheated on her or something or maybe he had a girl at his apartment and she caught him. Well, she drove us over there to his house. She left me in the car while she went to confront them. I could see them upstairs on his balcony screaming and pointing at each other. At one point there was a tussle and they were grabbing at each other. I must have stopped looking for a second when "BOOM!" there was a crash on the hood of our car. I swore I was going to look up and see her lifeless body laying across the front of the car. It ended up being her purse that she threw down but jeez, that moment has scarred me forever. Another time that same boyfriend had come over for dinner and my mom made this nice Italian dinner, spaghetti, homemade sauce and garlic bread. I was in the living room playing Nintendo and heard them start bickering. It started getting louder when I decided to come into the kitchen hoping they would see me and things would settle down. At the same moment, I see him throw a whole plate of spaghetti across the room into the wall. It shattered into a million pieces and drips of sauce were bleeding down the wall. I don't even remember if we ate dinner that night. Why does she put up with this crap? It seems like such a chore. If it were just the two of us, things probably would have been fine but all these guys do is make a mess and stress her out. I've never even seen my dad argue with anyone except for my mom and that's only over the phone and there is never any violence between them. They just can't stand each other. I hope these next couple of months give me a little break and maybe the break will be good for my mom too.

July 17, 1998

I've been here a couple weeks now and it's pretty cool. Except, it was my second day here and of course I got my period for the first time ever. Really? As soon as I move in with my dad?? He has no clue. I couldn't ask him for help.

We were out at a restaurant with my dad's friend Fabian. Thank God she is a girl. I had no idea what I was doing but she gave me a tampon. I've never even seen one of those things in my life—not out of the package anyway. It was all she had with her. She tried to talk me through using it and it got STUCK inside of me. I know it sounds gross and the whole experience was even worse than it sounds. What the hell?!?!! I was really embarrassed. What a way to start this new beginning.

I have my own room though and it's really nice. It looks like one of those rooms in the movies where all of the furniture matches. There is a cute, white, iron daybed and the room is full of these adorable blue and white ceramic decorations. It's not really made for a kid but it makes me feel fancy like I'm in a movie. I also love that everything goes together, not like my mismatched random furniture at home. He actually made space for me and was ready for me to come here. My dad even got me a job as a bus girl at the French restaurant where he works. It's called La Fourchette, the fork, weird. The owners are pretty tough but the lady seems to like me and I told her I want to learn French and my dad promised to take me to France one day. My dad and I laugh a LOT. It's fun working together. He taught me how to sneak in the walk in and eat the cold chocolate mousse puddings in 2 bites. The adrenaline of sneaking in there and trying not to get caught is off the charts. I think I've eaten one every night for the last week. I don't know what

I would do if the owner came in. Imagine having a mouthful of chocolate when she opens the freezer door. I would probably drop dead right there LOL. I could never show my face there again. Alright going to bed, got a long week of work!

July 20, 1998

Ewwww everyone thinks my dad is my boyfriend when we are walking around in public. He looks really young but that is gross. I mean, I guess my parents had me when they were 17 and 18 so we aren't that far apart in age. Still, my boyfriend?!?! Ew! We have never spent this much time together. It's nice that even though we work a lot we have time to go sightseeing and actually do stuff together. My dad still smokes cigarettes though. I haven't even touched cigarettes since last year and I can't stand the smell, especially when we are driving in the car together. I've been trying to hide them from him so he would stop or at least take a hint. I even broke a few but he got annoyed with that. I don't know why he smokes, it is actually pretty gross! Thankfully he doesn't really do it in the house, just the basement so none of our stuff smells like smoke.

August 11, 1998

    I feel like summer is almost over. I don't want to leave. I feel like a new person here. Something has sparked inside me and I'm happy again AND I haven't even been taking the happy pills. D.C. feels like a new start plus my dad doesn't yell at me or punish me all the time. Maybe I can ask my dad to call my mom about me staying here. I wonder if he wants me to stay here? Oh jeez, I hope he does. I don't want to give all of this back and go back to stupid Delaware with stupid chores and be in the same situation before I got here. Now that I've had this taste of freedom, a little glimmer of what it's like to make mistakes without being judged for every damn thing, I just can't go back. I'll never be the same.

August 19, 1998 ☆ ☆ ☆ ☆ ☆

    WE DID IT!!!! My dad called my mom and told her I wasnt coming home. Well, he made me say it first but then I just kind of threw the phone and refused to get back on. My heart was pounding and I thought she was going to come through the phone and grab me. Seriously, she got so mad on that call. I think at one point she was speechless. It didn't help that my dad was egging her on. He didnt even ask her. He just said, nope, she is staying with me. My mouth was wide open half the time and I was jumping and laughing hysterically. He seriously does not give a shit what she says. She tries to control him the same way she controls me but he doesnt let her. The more she pushes, the more he pushes back. Well, it worked in my favor thats for sure! She admitted defeat and said fine, but I'm not giving you her birth certificate or anything. You gotta figure out how to register her for school. Oooooh, you're really punishing him now. Doesnt she see that she is actually punishing me by doing stuff like that? It seems so childish. Whatever. I'm excited. I'm also getting to move my room down into the basement! It gives me more space and I can decorate. Now that I'm here for good I get to really make it my own.

August 30, 1998

Ahhhh! I didn't even get to tell you. They made me captain of the Junior Varsity cheer team at school! I think the other girls were pissed. I have literally no cheer experience but I came to all the pre-season practices, am organized and responsible. Plus I'm one of the few girls that actually comes on time and pays attention. It's nice to be recognized for that stuff but I still feel a little out of place. I'm not sure I really belong. Everyone here seems to know each other from middle school and I'm a bit of an outsider. Nobody is mean to me or anything. It's probably all in my head. Plus, having everyone stare at me in this short skirt is a little weird. I could do without the extra attention.

September 6, 1998

    I dont know what's going on. Things with my dad are NOT the same anymore. I feel a little bit like I was tricked. I don't think it was on purpose but things have changed so quickly now. I'm at school all day and he isn't even home when I get here. He works nights so I'm pretty much left to figure out what I'm eating for dinner. I have to walk to school but sometimes when it's raining I can convince him to drive me. It's only a few blocks but what girl wants to mess up her hair and have wet clothes going into school? My dad doesn't even ask about my homework or what I'm working on. It's a good change I guess but it just feels weird.

September 10, 1998

    This guy Shamar cornered me in the stairwell today. It was fuckin weird. I had my cheerleading outfit on because it's game day and nobody else was around. He kind of pushed me into the corner underneath the stairwell where the cameras cant see. He tried to put his hand up my skirt but I shoved it off and ran. It really pissed me off but I didn't know what to do. Who am I going to tell and what would they even say? I was just kind of scared. I definitely won't be going down that stairwell anymore.

September 16, 1998

    This new girl strolled in late to French class today
with her tight straight legged jeans, short choppy haircut
and a pair of Tims. She doesnt dress girlie but still has
this feminine look to her. I swear she didn't have a care
in the world. Everyone turned to look at her but she kept
her head high, grabbed an empty seat and shrugged her
shoulders as if she had no idea why all of our eyes were
glued on her. I was mesmerized. I'm not usually a rule
breaker but I could not pay attention to what the teacher
was saying. I was observing her every move. Halfway
through class she leaned over to me and asked if I wanted
a sip of some of her "water". She gave me a side wink so I
would know there was in fact no actual water in the bottle.
As soon as I opened the bottle I could smell it. DEFINITELY
ALCOHOL. I chuckled and declined to do shots of alcohol
at 9 in the morning! This girl had some guts I tell ya. A
moment later I was hoping she would ask again so I could
try it. I began to daydream about what it must be like to be
her. How can she just walk around and not give a fuck about
anyone or anything? And not in a careless way, maybe a
reckless way, but it wasn't that she didn't care. I'm sure she
has feelings but the thought of other peoples perceptions
clearly dont get in the way of what she wants to do at any
given moment. This was powerful. I tried to picture what it
was like to NOT have to walk around on eggshells — but to

LITERALLY bust into a room with your boots on and stomp around like you owned the damn place. Let me be clear. She didn't do this in an attention-seeking way. It's just that it demanded your attention because of her boldness and authenticity. I want that. I want to be that. I'm still in awe of that sparkle she has. Something is alive inside of her and I can't wait to figure out what it is.

September 20, 1998

Tamara and I have become really good friends. It's nice to have someone to depend on and we laugh hysterically together all the time. I think some of her confidence has rubbed off on me too. A few days after we first met in class, she grabbed my arm, interlocked it with hers and declared that we were now friends. I don't even think I had a choice in the matter! We have been stuck to each other like glue ever since. The other day we skipped last period and ran home to my house. We swore the security guards were going to see us going out the side door and chase us in their trucks. They were probably taking a nap! ha...Thankfully my dad was working tonight. I got the phone call from the school about my absence and just deleted it off the caller ID. Ok, well gotta go call Tamara and see what big plans she has for us tomorrow. TTYL!

September 27, 1998

Tamara has been making flirty comments to me about my cheerleading skirt. First I thought she was just joking and poking a little bit of fun at me because clearly she isn't a "cheer" girl either. She doesn't wear any makeup or even use scented lotions. That girl always has chapstick for her lips though! She has the best smile and an infectious laugh. She has these little gaps between each of her teeth that I think are so cute. She hates them but I think it gives her character, as if she needed it anymore! I actually think she kind of likes it when I come dressed up on game days. Maybe she will come watch the game this weekend.

September 28, 1998

We cut class again today to smoke a cigarette out in the woods. I know, I know. The damn cigarettes. I dont know what it is. I still don't like the smell but Tamara just makes it look so damn cool, like she doesnt have a care in the world. Tam loves the original Marlboros. I could only smoke half of one before feeling nauseous. Ugh, and I still hate that smell. I tried to cover it with spray and lotion. It's still probably in my hair. I haven't even seen my dad in a few days so I dont have to worry about him smelling it. I'm more worried about the teachers being disappointed in me. Fuck em though. They don't even know me. They probably don't even care. My dad did give me a cell phone the other day though. I was so excited. For a while I just had a pager and it was a pain to make sure I had change to call him back. He said now that I have a phone, if he calls me, I have to call him back, no matter what.

October 5, 1998

I slept over at Tam's house last night. Thankfully the school bus driver let me hop on her bus without asking any questions. We practically stayed up all night. Her mom is never home either so we spent the night smoking cigarettes in her room and taking pictures. She is in photography class so she has this nice camera. We played around with all these model shots and it was so fun. I love hanging out with her. She always makes me feel so pretty. Just being in her presence makes me feel a little more alive, ya know? My anxiety, the need to make everyone happy and my little rule following self seems to disappear a bit. It's like having a tiny taste of freedom. Most of the time I'm so worried about what others

think but with her, it's like I dont have to worry at all. She never pressures me or forces me to do anything so I know she accepts me no matter what. It's kind of nice.

October 15, 1998

We hung out at this laser tag place last night. Tamara's boyfriend Yuki works there. I think he is like 20 years old but he looks like a teenager. He is pretty cool plus he is the manager there so he let us all hang out on the front steps and the parking lot. Some of the boys were doing tricks on skateboards and smoking cigarettes. We played this arcade game called Area 51 too. I'm pretty good at it. I like beating all the boys.

It's weird, Yuki didn't look like I thought he would. I dont know what i thought he would look like but he had this soft side to him. I'm not sure he's the type of guy that can handle Tamara. She is pretty wild. I don't know why I think she needs to be "handled" but I just cant imagine the two of them being compatible. Half the time Tamara is in her own world. She always seems like she is having so much fun and it makes all of us around her want to have fun too. It still feels like she has a bit of a wall, like nobody can get really close to her or make her feel vulnerable. Maybe I'm just overthinking it and probably being self-conscious. Clearly she likes hanging out with me. We have been inseparable for weeks now.

October 16, 1998

I can't believe this happened! You know how I told you Tamara and I have been skipping classes sometimes? Well, today she pulled me into the girls bathroom at school and said she had to show me something. She poured out this white powder and lined it up on the back of the toilet. My eyes must have been huge! Then she rolled up a dollar and told me to snort it. I had no idea what I was doing and blew it with my breath all over the place. We were cracking up because I was so new to this. Then she showed me how to do it by plugging one side of your nose and using the dollar to suck in air through the other side. I tried it again and it was crazy. There was this nasty medicine drip in the back of my throat almost immediately. It almost gagged me! We had to hurry up before someone came into the bathroom but I felt like I was buzzing for the rest of the day! My body was tingly and I was in such a good mood. I can't believe I did it but honestly, I would do it again. It didn't seem like that big of a deal. It's not like its heroin. I would never do something that hard. Plus, cocaine seems like one of those classy drugs you know? She got it from Yuki so maybe we can try it again this weekend while we are driving around once he gets off work.

October 22, 1998

I like school but it's starting to get hard. Even though I have Tamara, I feel really alone like I don't have anyone I can count on. My dad is hardly home and even when he is, things are a bit chaotic. I don't know how to explain it but he always seems rushed or excited and because I don't get a lot of time with him, I feel like I should spend all of it with him when he is home. I feel like I'm growing up really fast. This last year has been a bit of a whirlwind with moving, new schools, getting my period, shaving, it's just a lot. And on top of it all, I dont feel like I have anyone to turn to. Do my parents even really care or know all of these things that are going on? Ugh, sorry to dump all of this on you. I just dont know if these feelings are normal or not. I'm so conflicted all the time. I want to be accepted and then I think I shouldn't care. I think I feel depressed but that feels stupid and I don't have any good reason to be so sad. I'll probably get over it. I'm just scared that this always happens and I don't want to take pills again or try to escape all of this.

November 2, 1998

We hung out with Yuki again last night. Hanging out with Tamara is like being in a movie! Late nights driving in the back of a car, riding fast, music blaring, shifting gears on the highway with the windows down and our hair blowing everywhere! Rolling up $20 bills and snorting lines of cocaine on a shimmery octagon shaped mirror. It all feels like a dream and a bit glamorous. Yuki plays the same CD nonstop by Lil Suzy. I'm gonna have to buy my own copy because I can't get the songs out of my head. Haha that's a bit ironic. The best song on there is called Can't Get You Out Of My Mind. "I can't get oh, I can't get oh, can't get you outta my mind, you make me feel so goooooood."

My dad listens to house/techno music like that too sometimes. I've never been to a rave but pretty sure people that do go to them would be spinning around with glow sticks while listening to it. That or maybe skating around at the skating rink.

November 11, 1998

I've been skipping classes a little more but it's ok because I've been trying to keep up with my work anyway. My dad hasn't even gotten any of the calls so he has no clue. Tamara has been letting me do a few lines with her and Yuki after school some days. It's kind of fun to hang in his bedroom and just talk while we are all high. Usually we ride around afterwards while Yuki makes a few stops and meets up with people. I assume it's pretty expensive so if he can sell it for more than he pays then we all get to do coke for free. Hahaha. I like these third wheel benefits. It does feel a little odd hanging out with them when they're kissing and holding hands but it's worth the slight awkwardness plus they don't seem to mind that I'm there.

November 15, 1998

I've been skipping out on full days of school at this point. I figure I'm already failing, so it can't get much worse. I can't believe I used to be on the honor roll. Pretty sure I'm failing every class at this point. Honestly though, I still have time to turn it around. I just don't see the point. Yuki has been meeting us outside of the school to pick us up before first period even starts. He just had his 21st birthday so now he can buy us alcohol too! I'm thinking of having a party at my house during Thanksgiving break so maybe he can hook us up.

November 23, 1998

Ahhhh it was so fun. I can't believe everything that happened but maybe the craziest thing that happened was with me and Tom! I know I haven't really told you about him but he hangs out at the laser tag place too plus he has a nice red car with a sound system. He isn't my usual "type" (whatever that is!) but he has this blond spiky hair and wears huge baggy jeans. He looks kind of like a skater boy yet I've never even seen him skateboard! I had that party in my basement last night. My dad was going to be out and he said he didn't care if I had people over so I invited a whole bunch of people over. Tom went and picked a bunch of people up from the laser tag spot and Yuki gave him some alcohol to bring. Everyone was just smoking and drinking in the basement while we blasted some music. We didnt pull out any coke at the party because that probably would have been a little too much. Nobody else knows I've been getting into that and I feel like Tom may have judged me or told me to stop. Tom and I were making out on the couch when things got a little heated. He asked if I wanted to go upstairs with him to my room. I was nervous but I definitely wanted some alone time with him and didn't want to seem like a prude. First we were just making out in the dark and touching each other. Then things started getting a little hot and heavy. He is a couple of years older than me so I figured it wasn't his first time. He asked me if I was a virgin. I told him the truth and he tried to stop and said we didn't need to go any further. I didn't want to stop though. It definitely was not what I expected and hurt like hell. He was trying to be gentle but that didn't happen. I wish someone had warned me about this.

I'm kind of excited to keep hanging out with him now. I don't know if we are really boyfriend/girlfriend but we've been talking for a while and I doubt it's going to stop now. Hopefully I see him tonight at the spot.

Soooo I guess I'm not a virgin anymore!

December 19, 1998

Ugh, I hope I didn't make a bad choice. Who am I becoming? Is this really who I am now? It feels big but maybe I'm just exaggerating. Tamara gave me a little bag of coke to take with me for the break since she knew I was going back to Delaware to visit my mom. Well...... I brought a little bit over to Suzanne's house for her to try. I didnt really think about it! I just wanted my friend to experience the same thing I did and I thought she would like it. I know she smoked weed before so it didn't seem like a big deal but now I'm hoping she doesnt judge me for it or even worse that she doesn't become as hooked as I have. I don't FEEL like I'm addicted but I definitely try to squeeze in all the time I can with Tamara and Yuki plus I'm always waiting for them to pull out that little bag. Suzanne seemed pretty shocked when I pulled it out. I tried to warn her but clearly I didn't do a good job. We only did a really tiny line so I don't even know if she felt anything. Plus I wanted to save some for later since I have a whole week here in hell.

February 12, 1999

I'm sorry it's been so long! Things have been crazy. I'll give you a quick update but basically my grades are awful and I've been missing a lot of school. Things with Tamara are great and I've been spending a lot of time with her and

Yuki. I'm not even sure she really likes him and honestly, he gets on my nerves too. What 21 year old wants to hang out with 14 year olds anyway? It's a little weird and creepy if you ask me. BUT, he does have the connect and I'm not sure we could get drugs any other way. I wonder if I could look in his phone and find out who he buys it from. I don't know, maybe that's too risky but I'm getting a little tired of his bullshit and I would rather just hang out with Tamara anyway.

May 15, 1999

DIARY!!! OH MY GOD!
   I can't believe this happened! Going to jail???? Yuki is going to jail!!! I've never known anybody who went to jail. It doesn't even seem real. I didn't even think this was a possibility. Thank God Tamara and I weren't in the car like usual. I was just getting ready for HFStival, waiting for her and Yuki to pick me up when Tamara called and said Yuki got picked up by the police and thrown in jail. What the hell??! Apparently he was driving around, dropping off drugs to all the locals before getting us when he got busted. They must have been watching him for a while because they waited until he had a large order on-hand and stopped him to search his car. Is that even legal? Why did they even pull him over? He does have really dark tinted windows and a big sound system so he was probably drawing attention to

himself. She said he was hiding the coke in lunch baggies inside of a Pringles container. He glued the paper top back on so it looked unopened but they found it. I don't even know what to do right now. My whole weekend plans are over. I mean I'm sad about Yuki and a little confused but I really wanted to see The Crystal Method and all the other bands at the concert. Maybe my dad can still get those tickets to the Tibetan Freedom Concert so I can see the Beastie Boys. That would be craaaaazy. Alright, well see you later. I'll probably be writing a lot more often now that I have NOTHING to do all summer and nowhere to go.

15 YEARS OLD

June 12, 1999

    I haven't heard from Tamara in a while. She lives all the way across town in Crystal City. Plus she doesn't even have her own cell phone. She usually calls me from her moms phone but sometimes it gets turned off so I just have to wait around for her to call. I guess I could take the bus and see her but I don't even think she wants to talk to me. I don't know. I feel like she blames me for what happened to Yuki or maybe it just isn't fun without the drugs. Damn, I just realized I haven't done any drugs in the last month. I thought people said you have withdrawals when that happens? Welp, guess I'm not an addict cuz I really didn't have any withdrawals. That whole life is behind me I guess. I do miss Tamara and the afternoon drives, sun shining down on us, hair in the wind with the windows down. Damn. There was something that made me feel free in those moments. Now I'm just ready for school to start back up again so I'm not so lonely. My dad said we might move again so I'll probably have to go to a different school......I was just getting used to this one, but maybe it will give me a fresh start. I just got my report card yesterday and have a 1.6 GPA! I'm lucky I didn't fail out of my freshman year. I've never had anything less than A's and B's. What a year.

BREAKING CYCLES

September 6, 1999

Freshman year was a doozy. 1.67 GPA which I'm pretty sure = failing. And now, just as I expected, I'm at a new school. We moved again. I'm a sophomore in this huge, new school. There are literally over 1,000 students here and 4 different languages on the wall. One good thing is that nobody even notices me. I just blend in with everybody. I almost failed out last year with all those times I skipped class with Tamara so maybe this is a second chance. I don't know why it matters anyway but I do want to do well in school. Alright, well gotta go do this homework. Talk later!

November 1, 1999

I got my working papers from school and a job at a bakery a couple of weeks ago. It's kind of cool cuz you get free food with every shift. I'll probably gain 10 lbs eating all of these sweets. I can only work like 15 hours each week but they put me on the schedule as much as possible. The only thing that sucks is I have to take the public bus to and from work. It's starting to get dark early and I'm not a big fan of hanging out at the bus stop alone at night. It's been keeping me busy though so that's good. Classes at this new school are a little harder too but I'm trying really hard. I actually do my homework and go to class now. I know, big surprise! The people are cool too but I haven't really found my group of friends yet. It's hard because I'm in so many different classes and the school is huge. It's not like I see the same people throughout the day. I love the diversity though. I guess because we are so close to Washington D.C. there are so many types of people from all over the world that live here. We have 4 different languages written on all the signs in our school. Alright, well off to sleep and do it all over again tomorrow.

December 16, 1999

Wow, looking back just last year, I feel like I was a whole different person. Skipping class, smoking, drugs, fast life. It's really a trip to think about how much I've changed. Sometimes I think it's a sign of strength but then I wonder if I'm just flaky and easily persuaded. Why is it that I can transform into this different person depending on who I'm with? I guess it's good I'm not with those people anymore.

March 3, 2000

I've been hanging back at the laser tag spot on the weekends. It's weird going there and Yuki doesn't work there anymore. There is a new crowd of kids. I met this kid Kevin last night. He gets homeschooled because he was caught with weed in his locker at his last school. I dont know if he was selling it or what. He seems pretty cool, skater vibe, smokes cigarettes sometimes but I think he's into me. We play around and act silly together. Most of us don't even play laser tag cuz it's so expensive there but they still have the arcade games. Now we live so close that I can actually walk there so I don't have to depend on a ride. Maybe I'll see him there again tonight.

April 2, 2000

Guess what? Kevin asked me to be his girlfriend! It was bound to happen. We see each other every weekend and I like hanging out with him. His parents are cool too. They let us hang out at his house a lot. Usually we just watch movies on his couch or go to the basement. His brother is kind of annoying but Kevin just yells at him to leave us alone. I think his mom really likes me. She invites me over for dinner a lot and is constantly asking us if we want food. They don't eat together or anything but it's always good food. They let us eat in the living room and watch tv. ♡♡♡

16 YEARS OLD

June 1, 2000

    I can't believe we moved again. I can never get comfortable. I was really starting to like that apartment. I had this huge room with these beautiful windows and I could see the whole city at night. Plus, my job at the bakery was pretty cool, even though I hated riding the bus home. It felt creepy when it was dark outside and I was always afraid I was going to have to fight for my life if some stranger tried to grab me. This place is a little ragged. It's a tiny ass one bedroom with a hallway kitchen and tiny living room. My dad has all his stuff and is sleeping in the living room but the bathroom is my room so he has to come in to use it. He is barely home anyway so I guess it makes sense. I don't even know why we had to move but it's like all of a sudden we picked up our stuff and moved out. I wonder what he did with all of that other furniture. I feel like I threw my stuff in some trash bags, we took my bed and a dresser and that was it. There is a corner store right across the street so that will make things easy but I don't even know the bus routes over here. At least I've been saving up for a car. I might head to the mall this weekend to look for a new job.

June 8, 2000

I got a new job at the mall. It's close to Kevin's house and our school. I can basically walk there after school and usually Kevin's parents drive me home at night or take me to their house to hang out for a while. I need to start saving money for a car, then I wouldn't need to rely on anyone for anything. Anyway, it's this clothing store. The clothes are pretty preppy and not really my style but I get a huge discount and it's pretty much the only way I can get new stuff.

July 14, 2000

I've been working at the clothing store for a while now. It's pretty cool but I HATE folding all the clothes at the end of the night. Every time someone comes in and they are picking up the shirts to look at every color and size, I start to cringe. And of course they just throw them down in a big pile without even thinking about it. Ugh. Oh well, at least I get paid every other week and I've got quite a bit saved up now. I also realized that when we get shipments in, I can just take a few things from the back stock and shove it in my bookbag before it gets cataloged. I know it's wrong to steal but it's not like I'm taking it from a person and I really do need the stuff. I feel like I've always been the girl with the old clothes or hand-me-downs and now I can finally have the trendy stuff but of course cant afford it really, even with this job. I can work a little more now in the summer but it's not like I can work a 40 hour work week and I'm hardly making minimum wage. Not to mention I'm paying for everything else I need like toothpaste and groceries. I feel a little bad still.

July 31, 2000

You'll never believe it! I got a car. It's a real piece of work but hey, it gets me where I gotta go. It's this cute little stick shift Honda Accord and only costs $1,000. Now of course I've gotta pay insurance and gas money but as long as I keep this job, that shouldn't be a problem. It's pretty clean inside too and now I wanna save up for a sound system. I don't need anything crazy but definitely a way to play CD's.

August 11, 2000

Jeez, yesterday was wild. I don't even know what to think anymore. I came home in the afternoon from work and my Dad was freaking out. He was having one of his cleaning fits where he fixes or rather breaks everything around the house while he claims to be fixing them. I don't know if it's a manic episode or what but it was scary. He didn't know what day it was and then was telling me that today's paper is actually yesterdays date and the world is trying to conspire against him to make him believe it's a different day. I called Kevin to come back over to my house and help me. I didn't know what to do. It didn't seem like he was drinking or this was something like that. It felt like he was going crazy. Shit, I felt like I was going crazy. I finally convinced him that we should go to the doctor or the hospital to get him checked out and make sure everything was ok. I thought maybe he hit his head and his brain was bleeding. The whole way to the hospital he was confused and then getting angry at Kevin. At one point he even spit in Kevin's face. I was mortified. I just kept driving until we got there. The lady at the front desk said I couldn't do anything and my Dad would need to check himself in. He finally broke down crying and said he would do it. I felt so scared and relieved at the same time. They said I couldnt come in for now and that they would keep him overnight for observation. Well, this morning he checked himself out and I have no information. He doesnt know what was wrong with him or what happened and now I'm just confused and worried. Am I supposed to do something? Does he need to see a doctor? Why did they let him out?

August 21, 2000

   I dont know if I should feel bad. How did I become a thief?? I took clothes from work today. I don't think it's that bad. It's not like I stole from a person. It's a store with probably millions of dollars annnnd I needed new clothes. I don't make enough money there to actually buy them myself. Yesterday we got a shipment in and I shoved a bunch of stuff in my bookbag. It was packed. I was so nervous someone was going to notice or check my bags before I left. I got a little greedy but I didn't know if I would get a chance to do it again so I wanted to stock up.

August 29, 2000

Kevin and I went to a huge concert last night. The last time I went to a big concert like that was Melissa Ethridge with my dad. I think I was 10 and had no idea what was going on. This time I was just as confused and a little bored to be honest. It was all the music he listens to. Honestly, I didn't even know most of the artists but the headliner was Pearl Jam and they had this guy Robert Plant make a cameo. I guess he's pretty famous because everyone loved him. Even though the music wasn't really my speed, it was cool to jam out to him playing guitar and Kevin was having a great time.

September 1, 2000

Here we go again. Another new freaking school, this is #3 for high schools. I wonder how many houses I've lived in my whole life now......I think it's 11. That's a lot right? I feel like most people live in like 1 or 2 houses their whole childhood and I've been in at least 11 and I'm not even 18 yet. Good thing I'm used to all these changes. Being the new kid doesn't even faze me at this point. This place is really nice but everyone already has their friend groups from middle school as usual and I'm just this weird outsider. A few of the popular girls have welcomed me to sit at their table in the cafeteria which was nice but I'm not sure I really fit in or if they are my people, ya know? It seems like everyone here grew up with money and is super smart. I'm in the honors classes too but I'm pretty sure I'm the dumbest one there lol. It feels like I'm drowning and struggling to keep up with the pace. Junior year is going to be rough. It's funny to think back to what things were like Freshman year to now. I'm pretty sure I've reinvented myself, well not on the inside, but at least to everyone from the outside. None of these people would EVER think I touched a drug in my life—let alone cocaine. It's kind of like my little secret, something I can keep to myself and I look like a damn straight-edger. Nobody at this school even suspected or would dream about me being that girl that I was, or that I am. Oh yeah, and Kevin is allowed back in school and goes here now so that's cool that we can see each other more during the week and not just on weekends.

September 22, 2000

I've been hanging with Hannah more. Even though she is the popular girl, I feel like she is really nice and welcoming to everyone. We are both on the colorguard/dance team together so we basically talk every day. We are doing this choreo to a Britney Spears song. It's going to be amazing. There are only 5 of us though and our band is huge! I hope it's not embarrassing being out on the field with everyone watching us. First game is coming up soon, I'll let you know how it goes.

October 22, 2000

I've been hanging with some of the girls in my classes and at lunch time. It's nice to finally have a group of friends to laugh with. This girl Hannah is definitely the popular girl. She is gorgeous, skinny, great skin, a beautiful smile and of course big boobs. The boys are obsessed with her. I talk to Keyaira the most. She is really down to earth and funny with a little dark humor. I like that she can be serious at times and talk about real shit, not just fluffy high school girl things. I'm finding out people at this school don't really seem to like Kevin. I don't know why but he rubs people the wrong way. The girls keep asking why I'm with him and are kind of shocked we are boyfriend/girlfriend. It's just nice to have someone I can depend on and because we are at the same School, I can just walk home to his house afterwards. His mom always makes dinner and his dad is nice too. His brother is kind of a jerk but is younger than him so Kevin just tells him to "fuck off". I guess he is just comfortable. I know he is always there, ya know? Who else would I hang out with or call if I didn't have him? I mean and it's nice to be wanted too. Another new day tomorrow. Good night.

November 11, 2000

Kevin and I have been arguing a lot. I don't know if it's just my jealousy or what. He is always making comments about girls on tv or saying we should watch this show because of some celebrity he likes. The other day we were bickering back and forth but trying to be quiet because everyone was home and he ended up stabbing my hand with a pencil to get me to shut up. I was so pissed. I got up to leave and was just going to find a way to walk home even though its way too far to walk. He convinced me to ride with him instead. Instead of driving me straight home he drove over to the cemetery where we always hang out. I really just wanted to go and was done talking but he was driving erratic and refusing to take me. Honestly, i was starting to get scared, especially with all these little violent things he has been doing. Not just the pencil thing but he has been pinching my arm when I say something in public he doesnt like or pulling my hair. We were in his moms van and I opened my door and was just going to jump out and roll. He grabbed my hand before I could actually go through with it and now I'm glad he did because how was I actually going to do that? I mean, once I rolled out of the car he could have just driven over me or chased me down with the damn car.

I need to leave him. This is getting too intense but I don't even know who to turn to. It's not like I can tell Kevin's mom what he's doing to me and the girls at school already hate him but how are they gonna help? Makes me think about all the bullshit with my mom. I could never figure out why she didn't leave some of these guys before but now I get it. It feels like you're stuck plus what is the other option? I dont even see any way out. It's just something you live with I guess.

December 29, 2000

Ahhh, we had the best party last night at Keyaira's house. Her brother is older so these college kids came and we were all just hanging out drinking, dancing and acting like idiots. The girls all spent the night in Keyaira's room. Her parents are gone for the whole weekend so we had time to clean everything up. That place looked immaculate! Hell, her parents are going to be suspicious because it's probably TOO clean. We must have had 5 trash bags of bottles. The boys were doing beer bongs and pounding their chest like typical guys. Some of the girls were smoking cigarettes but I still can't stand the smell, plus it's way too cold outside. We didn't let anybody drive home so it was cool that everyone could be safe and not have to worry about being too drunk. Man, I wish she had a pool, that would have been really fun! Christmas break is almost over, I can hardly believe it and soon we are going to be seniors. I need to start looking for colleges soon, jeez.

January 8, 2001

Kevin and I broke up today. I guess I broke up with him but I don't even know how I had the guts to do it. We were just screaming and arguing and I guess now that I have a group of friends at school it made things a little easier. I know these girls have my back and the fact that everyone at school has a problem with him says something. He isn't just a jerk to me. We were so toxic together. I was sick of the arguments and back and forth. It was nice to have someone all the time but then we would fight and scream over everything. I was so jealous all the time and I think he liked it. I don't feel like I'm insecure but it felt like I always compared myself to all the celebrities and movie stars he had a crush on. He even had these stupid sports illustrated posters on his walls in his room. Like why do you have to look at that all the time? And then I'm supposed to feel confident when we are having sex or being together? Ha!

Yeah right.

It was like he wanted me to be jealous of him looking at other girls. Keyaira and Hannah were happy for me too once I told them it was over. It had to be done. Now maybe I can get closer with them. None of them are really dating anyone so it was always me who had a boyfriend and I felt like I had to choose a lot. Now all I have to worry about is myself!

January 27, 2001

FINALLY the security guard let us out for lunch today! They don't usually let the juniors leave but this one guard has been cool. He lets our whole group go out. I think it's because he knows we are coming back. It's not like we wanna skip school. We literally just go to Taco Bell then get back in time before our next class. Oh there is this amazing Peruvian chicken spot too that everyone goes to. They have this sauce for the chicken that is so good! I hope we go there tomorrow.

March 6, 2001

School is getting hard. We have PSATs coming up soon. I'm kind of nervous. Everyone in my classes seems so smart, and it's like I have to WORK for it. It doesn't just come naturally like it does for all of them. It's been hard finding as much time to study and get homework and essays done, but thankfully all of us are in the same classes pretty much, so after school, we hang out at someone's house. Not my house, of course! There wouldn't be enough room. I literally live in a single bedroom, small bathroom, hallway kitchen and tiny-ass living room. I don't know how much 1,000 square feet is, but it's gotta be smaller than that, and there are 2 people and a cat living there. All of my friends have these huge family homes with like 4 bedrooms and a front and a backyard. I basically live in the damn projects, though I don't think it's free. My dad pays some kind of rent, or at least I hope he does. If he doesn't, we will probably be moving again next year. Now that I think about it, I've never had any of them over the house except for Kevin when we were dating before. That would just be embarrassing, and they probably would think I'm even weirder or feel bad for me, and I don't need anyone doing that.

study! study! study! study!

May 11, 2001

I can't believe I didn't tell you! I started dating this guy, Vinh. We have been friends for a while, but it just kind of happened out of nowhere. He's an emo kid and not really like any guy I've dated before. He is funny and silly and actually treats me pretty well. That's a shocker! He made me a mixed CD the other day. It was so sweet. It had all these songs with super cute lyrics. I feel like a bit of an imposter. I don't know how to explain it, but it's like I'm a completely different person on the outside with him. I still feel like myself in my head, but I started changing my clothing style and music choices. I even started wearing less makeup. It's all good stuff, I guess. It's like I'm shedding my old skin and getting to start over. Hopefully this lasts.

June 7, 2001

We went to a concert last night. It was so fun and dirty
and sweaty. It was this little back alley place in Baltimore.
There was this grittiness about it. I felt like we were in a
secret spot nobody knew about—some underground-type
shit. The band is called The Stryder, and I'm obsessed now.
I loved all the songs, even the ones I didn't know the
lyrics to. This one song is fun to sing, and every time I act

The Stryder!

out the lyrics. I probably looked ridiculous, but I don't even care. I was singing at the top of my lungs, "This aint my styyyyyyle, it's just a disguise. Here is my face, where are my eyyyyes? I'm on my skateboard, frozen in tiiiiime." I act out every line, and of course, you gotta get your voice deep and low for the "frozen in time" part. Woah, woah, waaaoooooohhh. I'm still closing my eyes, jammin out to the songs on repeat while writing this.

I think I'm hooked. I bought the EP and almost got a t-shirt but didn't want to go crazy. A girl has gas to pay for! There were legit only 30 or 40 people there, which made me a little nervous cuz most of them were adults, and here we were, some little teenagers hanging in a bar. Got a pic with the band too, so that was cool.

11:11 See ya!

July 25, 2001

Fuck Michelle Branch. I've been getting so jealous lately. Vinh loves this chick, but her music is mediocre at best. It's a bunch of pop songs. She literally sounds like every other artist on the planet. Shit, I'll take Brittney or Christina over her any day. And of course, just like every other boy on the planet, he has a freaking poster of her on his wall. I don't know why it bothers me so much. I keep getting annoyed and then arguing with him about it. Like, why don't you just take it down? You have a freaking girlfriend.

I don't know. He jokes around so much and doesn't take my feelings seriously at all. Kevin has been reaching out a lot recently too. I guess he feels bad for all the shit we went through. It is nice to be wanted, and I'm not even sure Vinh cares if I come or go. He just sings his songs and writes his poems all day long. I used to think the poems were for me, but really, I think he just likes fantasizing and writing love songs.

August 1, 2001

Don't be disappointed in me, but we broke up. I couldn't take it anymore, and I have too much other shit to worry about than to be arguing and bickering with some guy about if he loves me enough or not. He probably thinks I'm a psycho with this jealousy stuff, but I can't be worried if you're fantasizing about some other girls while we are together. What's the point? You either want me or you don't. Clearly, he DON'T!

August 11, 2001

Yesterday was the best and worst day all in one. My freaking car broke, and now it won't idle by itself. Basically, it just shuts off unless I keep one foot on the gas. So now any time I'm in park or at a red light, I have to keep my right foot on the gas so it idles and my left on the brake.

Don't even get me started on how I have to shift gears to get into first. I don't even know who I would call to fix this, and they would probably just screw me over since I'm a girl. Not to mention it probably costs a million dollars to fix. I'm gonna have to find a way to get a new car eventually.

Oh, so anyway, the best part is that I met Kevin at the park, and we decided to give it another go. I'm excited this time is going to be different. He promised not to do weird violent shit anymore, so I'm hopeful he will keep his word. It's nice his mom lets him drive her van everywhere, and he usually holds my hand while he is driving. It's kind of sweet. The only bad part right now is he smokes cigarettes all the time, and honestly, I can't stand the smell anymore. Who the heck smokes Marlboros? I thought those were for old people. Well, that is the kind his dad smokes, so that's probably why. Heading to bed with a smile on my face! :)

September 11, 2001

Today has been the most insane day. I'm glad I have Kevin because today was scary. They locked us down in the school and wouldn't let us leave. Nobody's cell phones worked at all. Kids were crying and so worried about their parents because everyone here works somewhere in DC. I don't even know what's happening in our country. People were screaming and crying and begging security to let us out. They said the school was a safe haven, and we had to stay because we were under attack. Nobody's cell phones worked, and everyone was freaking out because half of the school's parents work in Congress or the city close to the Pentagon. It all started in first-period English class. Someone said a plane hit the World Trade Center, so our teacher turned on the TV in the room so we could watch the news. We turned it off after a few minutes and went to our writing assignment, but then we could hear people yelling in the hallway. When we turned the TV back on, we saw ANOTHER plane hit the Pentagon. At that point, there was no more school. In every class, we just watched the news in horror and saw people jumping from the smoking buildings. My dad works at night, so I wasn't worried, but my mom was trying to call me and couldn't get through. She was freaking out. I went to Kevin's house after school, and we just watched the news for hours. Nobody knew what to say. I wonder what those people were thinking when they jumped. How desperate they must have felt to have to end it that way. It's just really sad. I don't think we will have school tomorrow. Kevin and I talked about going to the Pentagon to help the Red Cross people clean things up outside the building. Well, I'm tired. I'm going to go to bed. Talk to you tomorrow.

October 3, 2001

On again, off again. It never stops! Kevin and I have no idea what we are doing. I keep getting sick of his games and breaking up with him, then he coerces me back into his vicious web. I don't know what it is, but I can't get away from this dude. It's like he has a hold on me. It's not like I don't have anyone to hang out with, and all my friends keep telling me to leave him. I haven't even told them all of the insane stuff he has done in the past, like when he stabbed me with that pencil and tried to leave me stranded at the park. He knew damn well I had nobody to call to pick me up. I guess I could have called Hannah, but that would have been embarrassing.

November 6, 2001

So I don't know if I told you, but I'm in the International Baccalaureate program at school. I know it sounds fancy, but it's not! I can hardly pronounce the word, but I guess they thought I was smart enough to be in these honors classes. Everyone calls it IB for short because nobody wants to say that ridiculous word. I'm barely hanging on in these classes. And then AP History is absolutely absurd. There is so much reading and tons of essays to write. I can't remember or understand what I'm reading half the time. Oh, and I submitted all of my college applications the other day. I'm clueless about what the heck I'm going to do, where I'm going to go, and what major I would even want. I did send an application to Johnson and Wales, the one in Rhode Island. They have this insane culinary program. My dad always talked about wanting to own this little cafe called "The Park," and I think it would be pretty cool. We could probably run it together. I can picture it now. This cute little spot with small round tables and iron rod chairs. Not uncomfortable ones but the kind I imagine you would see in Paris.

Thank goodness I retook my SATS this year. Last year was abysmal—see what I did there? Using those big IB words, LOL. This time I finally broke 1200, but my math score sucked, so we'll see what happens.

November 26, 2001

Welp, I did it. Finally broke up with Kevin. This time it's for good. Screw that guy. We were stuck together like glue, but all we did was argue. I'm still sad about it, but not because I love him or anything. I mean, we did say I love you, but I just miss knowing he was always there, ya know?

January 20, 2002

Ahhhhh, you'll never believe it!!!!! I got my acceptance letter back from Johnson and Wales, and they want to give me a full ride basically! I have to maintain a B average, but they will literally pay for me to go there. I would have to find a way to cover housing, but I'm so hyped. I applied at a bunch of other places still, so I want those to come back first. A lot of my friends are going to UVA, but I'm pretty sure it's hard to get into, and we already know I'm the dumbest one out of the group of smart kids at my school, so that probably ain't happening. Wish me luck anyway. I'll let you know soon, I hope.

February 1, 2002

Vinh made me a mixed tape, well, a mixed CD, but it was so cute. It had a bunch of our favorite songs and some new ones. We started talking again recently and decided to get back together. I did miss our car rides blasting music and riding around A-town. He has been super sweet, and we just hold hands and make jokes. He still talks to all the girls, and that's a little annoying, but I guess he is just a flirt in general. I mean, he's with me, so I really don't have a need to be jealous.

March 5, 2002

I finally made my choice for college. Vinh also got accepted into Virginia Tech, and it's not too far from home, maybe 6 hours, so we can come back and see all of our

friends pretty easily during breaks. I'm so excited. They
don't have a culinary major, but I figure I can take business
classes and learn how to run a restaurant. I mean, I
already know how to cook, and if I went to Rhode Island,
we would never see each other. I don't want to be alone in
a new city and have to start all over again. I can't believe
it's all happening. Graduation isn't far away, and
then it's like I get to start a whole new
chapter. Let's go Hokies!!!

April 3, 2002

   There is no food in the house again. My dad is never
even home for dinner anymore. I liked it when he used to
cook these elaborate meals and put them on fancy plates.
It always felt exotic when he would add garnish and
seasoning to give it a pop of color. Now he's never even
here. The house is a mess, and he sleeps in the living room
since I have the only bedroom. I try to keep it clean, but he
has so much stuff there is no way to even keep it clean. I
grabbed some groceries from the 7/11 down the street today.
I'm glad it's so close that I can walk pretty easily. It's not
the best area, and I'm pretty sure we might be living in
the projects, but it works for now, and what am I going to
do anyway? I still miss that old apartment in Fairfax with
the big window. That place gave me some hope. Now, I just
feel like we are poor again. I've always felt like the poor

kid. I can't wait to save up some money and choose my own destiny.

May 12, 2002

Prom was the best!!! I wore this beautiful white dress and felt like a million bucks! I looked like I was getting married, LOL, but I didn't care. Vinh and I were super cute. His parents took tons of pics of us together, and all of our friends got together to take group pics. It was straight out of a movie scene—the girls all lined up on one side of these winding steps outside surrounded by flowers and greenery and the boys on the opposing side all suited up. We literally danced ALL night. As soon as the beat dropped for back

PROOOOOMMMM!!!

that azz up, we all went wild, yelling at the top of our lungs, "CASH MONEY RECORDS TAKING OVER FOR THE 99 AND 2000S!" Then, of course, we hiked up our gowns, kicked off our heels, and backed our asses up. At the end of the night, there was dirt and grime along the walls from everyone sweating and dancing. The teachers must have been horrified. The seniors from last year were home from college and had a party, so of course we went to the after-party and got drunk. I don't even remember how I got home or what time it was, but it was the best night ever.

Back that azz up!

18 YEARS OLD

June 16, 2002

So glad school is out! There are so many summer concerts in Baltimore and Philly. I don't have to worry about any more damn papers to write or homework to finish. Now I gotta figure out all this college stuff. I filled out the FAFSA paperwork, so hopefully I get a few grants or scholarships, but I'm definitely gonna have to get a loan to pay for this. It's gonna be crazy, but I can't wait.

ADAM FROM TAKING BACK SUNDAY ♡

July 22, 2002

This sucks so much. The best summer ever turned into the worst, most boring summer. I went to see my favorite band of all time last night, Taking Back Sunday, and I basically broke my neck. Okay, well, I didn't break it, but I have to wear a damn neck brace. I look absolutely ridiculous. We were in the front row and people were doing their normal thing shoving everyone all around and moshing. I guess someone was crowd-surfing from behind me and the people couldn't hold them up so they ended up literally landing on my head. I must have fallen to the ground because I don't remember much after that. BUT I DO remember the lead singer Adam coming over and holding my hand while I was on the stretcher. That shit was crazy. Im lucky the mob of people didn't trample me. Vinh was there with me too and they let him ride in the ambulance with me. I'm gonna hang at his house for a couple of days. I can't spend the night but his mom always tries to take care of me and feed me, LOL.

PART 2: STRUGGLE

DARKEST NIGHTS

August 2, 2002

I'm so excited. I can't believe this is really happening. College is just around the corner, and I get to be there with my boyfriend. Ah, I feel like it's going to be a new start. There is no more Kevin and Vinh drama. I only know like 5 people who are going to Tech, but there are thousands more people that I can get to know. I just feel like things are finally going to be different. Oh, and did I mention both of my parents are driving me down together? That just seems crazy to me, LOL. I don't think I've ever been together with both of them, especially in a car, for 6 hours ever in my life!

August 8, 2002

My grandmother let me buy her Mazda M3. It's the cutest car ever. Literally my favorite color—that greenish blue with a sparkle. It's stick shift, of course, and just the cutest little hatchback. I feel like a badass driving it. Maybe that's weird, but I don't think many people my age know how to drive stick anymore, and shifting through gears, especially while in traffic, gives me that little adrenaline pump. Pluuuuuus, it's a lot better than that piece of crap I had before. Who knew it could be cool to drive your GRANDMA'S car?!! hahaha

August 17, 2002

I can't believe she tried me today. I'm fucking 18 and moving out on my own. Hell, I've basically been living on my own for the last 4 years. She and my dad drove me down to VTech today to help me move my stuff into the dorms and drop me off. She made one of her bitchy comments, and I must have gotten smart and said something back to her. Well, she threatened to smack me across the face right there in the middle of the campus in front of everyone. All the rage I've been holding onto for years boiled up into my face. I was crouched down on the ground picking up some of my stuff when I looked at her, dead in the eyes, and told her, "I fucking dare you!" At that moment, I was begging her to slap me. Oh, the things I would have done afterward. I can't believe she had the audacity to think she could still control me like she used to. I'm not your little girl anymore. I take care of myself now, and you certainly can't take care of me, not sure you ever did. Well, she didn't say a word. I think she was as shocked as I was that the words actually came out of my mouth. We carried about the rest of our day acting as if nothing happened, the same way we always do.

Now I'm just so happy to be here! I have my room all set up and met my roommate Kim earlier. She seems cool, and I think we will get along. I'm not even nervous, just excited to finally be here and truly start living my own life. The campus is huge though, so I gotta figure out where my classes are and figure out where everything is. Eeeeek! It's all happening.

August 29, 2002

Sorry I haven't been writing a lot. There has been so much drama between me and Vinh. I thought with us both being here we would be together all the time, just like we were in high school. I hardly even see him, though. He is always busy hanging out with his roommate or his new friends. All of that is fine and everything, but why not just invite me too? I'm sure he is doing his usual flirty stuff, and the girls on campus are absolutely gorgeous. I can hardly blame him.

August 30, 2002

I'm livid. Vinh and I have a class on the same side of campus around the same time. Well, I'm walking back to the dorm and see him walking with this girl. She reminds me of this same girl he dated before me in high school, and I started seething on the inside. I didn't even approach them.

I just broke down in tears and went back to my dorm. I tried calling him like 15 times, and he wouldn't even answer. He finally called me back and was so chill, acting like it wasn't even a big deal. I called that shit off right then. He literally never makes me feel like I matter. Okay, maybe it was nothing and you were just walking with a girl, but why not walk with me? Did you even think about me? No, never; he just lives in his own world. It's so frustrating. So I guess I'm single now. Thankfully, Kim and our dorm neighbor Rebecca got some alcohol, and we are playing cards and then going to the bar tonight. Apparently, there is some Coyote Ugly contest, so we're gonna see what it's all about.

Cuz you could slit my throat
And with my one last gasping breath,
I'd apologize for bleeding on your SHIRT! — TBS

September 8, 2002

Welp, I did it! I got my first tattoo today. It's this little blue butterfly on my lower stomach. You know that nervous and giddy feeling when you're falling in love or have a crush on someone? I wanted to remind myself to always feel that feeling. I don't think it should ever go away. If you're in love and care about someone, they should always give you butterflies. I feel like with Kevin and Vinh, I lost that feeling a lot. I mean, I only ever felt it in the beginning or when we would break up and get back together, but for the most part our whole relationship just felt like stress and drama. I'm not settling for that anymore. I want to always feel the butterflies.

September 30, 2002

I finally got the pictures printed from our Coyote Ugly night downtown!! I can't believe I did that. I would never imagine myself dancing on a bar, LOL. Some of the girls were getting really wild with white t-shirts and spraying themselves with the water gun. Of course, that one girl won the contest, but I was just proud of myself for even getting up there and trying.

We're taking it easy tonight, playing spades and asshole. Yesterday we went to a frat party, and I had to save Kim. That girl was

COYOTE UGLY DANCE CONTEST

wasted, and I was worried one of the guys was going to do something with her. She kept disappearing, and I felt like I was on mom duty all night.

October 1, 2002

I can NOT get to this 8 AM class. I don't know why I picked this schedule or what I was thinking?!?! I had no idea Thursday nights were going to be so fun. We go out every week, and of course, I stay up too late, and we're drinking. So getting up early on a Friday and hiking across campus to make it to class on time is not happening. Don't even get me started on my statistics class. I have to go to these extra tutor sessions, and it's embarrassing. I'm struggling to stay up and study and get my work done, but there are a lot of distractions.Of course, Kim is just wilding out, having guys over here every other night.

October 19, 2002

I really thought this roommate thing was going to work out, but this girl is getting on my nerves.

I started working at this place called the Farmhouse. Well, I have to walk like a mile to go get my car from the freshmen parking lot, work a whole night shift, and then walk back. I get to the dorm, and she has the door locked with a fucking sock on the handle. Apparently, this was her sign not to come in because she is screwing some guy. I spent an hour waiting in the lounge before I could finally get into MY OWN ROOM. I was pissed, but I didn't even say anything to her. I'm so over it. And I think she keeps using my shampoo and body spray. She could at least ask. I wouldn't mind, but she is so disrespectful.

October 21, 2002

I met this guy named Jason. He was at open mic night and played guitar. He sings these cute Jason Mraz cover songs. It's cute, and he is super nice. He asked to take me on a date. I don't think anyone has ever asked me on a date before, LOL. Usually, it's just meeting someone, we become obsessed with each other, hang out every second of the day, and then become boyfriend and girlfriend. Maybe this will be different. Who knows?

November 20, 2002

Okay, maybe I'm going boy crazy, or I'm just an idiot. The stuff with that guy Jason didn't work out. I mean, he was nice and everything, but I was so bored. It was almost like he was too nice. Like, do you even want me if you aren't fighting with me? LOL. Okay, that does sound crazy, but I just couldn't. We had nothing to talk about. Plus, Kevin and I started talking on MySpace again. He goes to William and Mary, but it's not that far. He said he's going to come visit next weekend, so we will see what happens. I'm kind of excited.

December 1, 2002

My entire life is drama!!! Why??? I seriously don't want it to be this way. I just want a guy who cares about me and loves me. So, Kevin came to visit me at Tech. The campus is huge, but of course, Vinh sees us, and it starts this whole nonsense of drama. Kevin is yelling across the field like he's going to beat him up. Vinh is laughing hysterically and egging him on. I don't even know why Vinh cares. He was done with me anyway. He should just go back to his little girlfriend and leave me alone. Then, he wrote me this long message about how disappointed he was and that I could do better, blah, blah, blah. Get out of here. So annoying.

December 21, 2002

I'm heading back home for winter break to Delaware to visit my mom and the rest of our family. I think my cousins will be there, too. I'm pretty excited to see everyone. Hopefully, we play board games and sit in the kitchen laughing. I remember when we used to do that all the time. Things with my mom seem easier now that I'm not living with her every day. Plus, I'm an adult now, so she can't really tell me what to do.

December 27, 2002

Ah, Christmas was nice. We did play games, and everyone was joking and laughing. My uncles are always making fun of me. It used to make me really self-conscious, but now I just laugh with them. We played this one game called "Babble On," where the words look like nonsense, but when you say them fast, they sound like something else. We were cracking up! Things felt a bit normal and calm for once. I don't think I've laughed that hard in a while, so it was nice for a few days. Plus, my mom and I were cool. I guess we were both in good moods and happy to see each other. They do say absence makes the heart grow fonder!

December 30, 2002

This shit with Kevin is never gonna work. We ended up breaking up over winter break. We just argue too much. I don't even know what we argue about. Maybe it's the long-distance or the jealousy stuff. I don't know, but it's stressful. It doesn't help that we are both freshmen in college, surrounded by tons of new people. I'm not the type to look at other people when I'm in a relationship, but he's a guy and can hardly control himself. Who knows what he is doing when I'm not around? I see these gorgeous girls at

Tech, and they are just as pretty at William and Mary. No way he isn't flirting, or hell, probably cheating on me when I'm not around.

January 2, 2003

What a fucking year. Welp, here we are kicking off January with another year of bullshit. How are you supposed to say "Happy New Year" to everyone when it's not happy AT ALL? I almost failed out of freshman year in the first semester because of an 8 AM Friday lab class (rookie mistake!), that damn statistics class made my head spin, and my roommate decided to sleep with every guy on campus.

January 17, 2003

Moving to a new dorm was the last straw. Lugging all of my shit across campus by myself was a nightmare. It was like the ultimate WALK OF SHAME, except I didn't sleep with anyone! Kim was the one sleeping with the whole town. Jeez. Just me and my bags and all my stuff lugged all the way across campus.

How did I even get to college, anyway? I'm pretty sure I never belonged in those honors classes back in high school, and somehow I made it through without anybody noticing. I shouldn't be here.

January 22, 2003

Looking back at the beginning of this school year, I really wish I had left both of those boys alone. What was I clinging to? What was I looking for? Trying to be everything they needed just held me back. I didn't spend as much time getting to know my new friends. I couldn't focus on my classes and homework, and it just brought me so much stress trying to make everyone happy. If only I could go back in time, I would have shaken myself and dropped both of them before school even started!

February 15, 2003

I've picked up so many shifts at the Farmhouse that it's ridiculous. I'm basically working a full-time job now and struggling through 19 credits. I'm an idiot for making this schedule. I always do too much. On the flip side, what else would I be doing with my time? Ahese student loans aren't going to pay themselves!! I literally have to walk a mile to get my car every day I work, and when I get home it's dark and scary. They don't even have the buses running at that time, so it's not like I can do that. It's all very inconvenient. The other day I almost sliced my damn thumb off cutting this box of chicken breasts. I sliced a piece off so clean that just seeing the blood made me woozy. I was going to just wrap it up and stay, but they sent me home and told me to go to urgent care. I had my little piece of thumb in a baggy, and I looked insane. The nurse kind of laughed and said there was nothing they could do with that. I'm glad I can go back to work tomorrow, though. I like being in the kitchen. It's like you don't have time to think about anything else with all of the orders coming in, and it's almost like a symphony when everything flows perfectly together and the back of the house is just vibing.

March 11, 2003

I think I messed up. Well, not really, but this young guy at work talked about partying. He asked something silly, like if I "enjoy playing in the snow." Well, we all know what that means, so I nodded my head yes. I think he was surprised. Most people would never look at me and think I've done drugs before, and certainly not snorting lines all day as a damn 14-year-old. That's crazy. I haven't touched the stuff in so long, I barely remember how to roll up a dollar. Well, of course, he told me if I ever want anything to hit him up.

March 15, 2003

Ahhh, Ryan got that stuff for me, and it was almost exactly like I remembered. I waited until I got home from work, then crushed up half the bag and laid out some lines. I wasn't sure what my tolerance was going to be like, but it had been so long that I was buzzing after just a couple of small lines. It kind of sucks doing it alone, though. I mean, I can't talk to myself, LOL. I'm not driving around outside, and there is literally nothing to do in my dorm room. It was nice, though. It's cool to know I have a connect when I need it. I'm definitely not going to get into the same routine as before, but I don't think it's so bad on the weekends. Plus, I'm working all the time or doing school stuff. I can't afford to do it every day.

April 19, 2003

Dear Diary,
WHAT THE FUCK WAS I THINKING?!?! I had the worst night ever. I spent it puking my guts out, thinking I was going to DIE alone in my dorm. Okay, maybe that's dramatic, but I wasn't sure it was ever going to end. Ryan gave me some oxy (or whatever the fuck they are called) last night and told me they were like coke. Ummm, no, they weren't! It was this little pill, so I smashed it up and snorted a

couple of lines. First off, they burned like hell, and there was no smooth drip in the back of my throat. Right away, I felt nauseous, and the entire room was spinning. I've never been that dizzy in my life. Thank God I have a little sink in my room because I was puking in that thing all night. I can't even figure out why people like these. I felt like a damn zombie. Once I finished barfing my guts out, I just felt empty, a bunch of nothingness. I could barely move, and I'm pretty sure I stared at the ceiling for half the night before passing out. It was not my idea of a fun Saturday night, that's for sure. Now I regret ever asking him for anything.

April 30, 2003

Work, work, work, work, work!! I'm barely hanging on this year. I did drop down to 15 credits, though. I'm pretty sure I'm going to have a withdrawal on my transcript for that math class because I did it late and that stupid lab I could never make it to. Whatever, I can't even care anymore. This is just the best I can do right now.

May 1, 2003

Is this how everyone's first year at college goes? I'm so damn lonely and depressed. I don't get it. It's not like I'm homesick. I just feel ALONE. ALONE! ALONE! ALONE! Me, my thoughts, and criticisms—all of which are terrifying and dangerous. I DO feel like I'm good enough, smart enough, and cool enough, but at the same time, I guess I'm not, or maybe others just don't see it. How am I failing all these classes and have nobody to really talk to or hang out with? Ugh, I'm going to bed.

MY NEW "ROOM" BACK HOME

May 12, 2003

Well, I came home yesterday, and all of my stuff was in big black trash bags in the living room. Of course, my dad moved again while I was at college and got a two-bedroom apartment with a friend, so I'm in the living room, I guess???

I don't even have a bed—just a mattress on the floor. He did bring my tall dresser, but I have no privacy. The place is actually nice and huge, but there are only 2 bedrooms, so I don't know how 3 grown adults are gonna live here all summer.

May 15, 2003

I don't know what the fuck I was thinking. Nobody was home, and I stared at the edge of the balcony, contemplating what would happen if I jumped. I tried for a while, hyping myself up, reminding myself nobody would really give a fuck. I mean, they would be sad, but would they reeeeally care? Plus, I'm too fucking sad, and it's not like anybody can help or fix it. I sure as hell don't know how to make it stop. Then I started picturing my dead, lifeless body on the sidewalk and other people having to see me like that. It would probably be traumatizing, and I just knew there was no way I would be able to climb up the railing and literally jump. Maybe if there was a way I could walk along the edge and fall, then I could have done it.

Well, after that failed, I started thinking of all the other things I could do. Clearly, I don't have a gun, so that wouldn't work. I know damn well I could not slit myself with a knife. Maybe I could get one wrist slit, but then I would chicken out. I went digging through all the cleaning supplies and found antifreeze. It had this huge warning about how poisonous it was. Plus, it's this pretty bright blue color, so I figured it would be easy to drink. I poured it into a glass and tried to chug it. Ummm, no. That stuff is so NASTY. I could barely get one gulp down. It sounds stupid, but I was a little disappointed in myself. I literally can't even kill myself. How do you fail at dying?? What a dummy.

May 22, 2003

I got a new job at this restaurant downtown. It keeps my mind off the nonsense, and I can stay busy. Everyone there is young, and I've been hanging out with this guy Tosh and some of the other people who work there. Tosh is cool. I like that we can be friends and it's nothing romantic. I can tell he isn't trying to get with me or anything weird. We just laugh and vibe at work. Oh, and he has the powder connect, so that's kind of nice. I've been trying not to do any lines at work, but literally everybody does it, and nobody seems to care.

What is it about these bathrooms? I feel like I'm always doing lines on the back of a toilet. Isn't that kind of gross? I guess it's clean, plus it's private and I can lock the door, but man, it just feels weird. I miss the good ole days of a chill living room vibe, a nice clean mirror, and freshly rolled $20 bills. Take me back to those days.

May 30, 2003

Happy birthday to me! You already know what I'm getting into today...

cocaine

coke

snow

powder

white stuff

white girl

blow

yayo

dust

19 YEARS OLD

June 2, 2003

I started looking at places to move. I found this spot in Fairfax on Craigslist and went to meet the guy who lives there. He is pretty chill. I basically get the whole first floor, and he lives in the basement apartment. We share common areas like the living room and kitchen, but we both have different schedules, and I would have my own room and bathroom. It's really nice and has a cute yard. I would probably get a job closer to the house, though, because I'm not trying to drive 30—40 minutes to work every day, especially not for these shitty tips.

June 15, 2003

I was just thinking today that this is like the 15th time I've ever moved in my life. Shoot, it might be 17 if you count moving into the dorms and then moving AGAIN into the second dorm room.

I made my room really nice, though, and I love the living room area. I can actually have company over now and get some damn privacy, too!

June 22, 2003

Tosh and I went to Ocean City for the weekend. It was so much fun. There are so many stories to tell, but mainly we went to the 18+ foam clubs. It was a blast. It's nice not paying for school right now, and I don't have that many bills besides my car and rent. Of course, I always have extra to get a bag for the weekend, too. Whenever Tosh and I hang out, we both just share whatever we have. Nobody is pressed or worried about how much anyone is doing. I remember I hated that with Yuki. I always felt like I had to do less and didn't like asking for another line. Now I'm in control and can do whatever I want when I want. Boom.

July 1, 2003

I got a new job! It's at this restaurant/bar that also has pool tables. Definitely an older crowd, but everyone is super nice. They serve all kinds of specialty chili, and people drink a lot of beer. Tips are decent, plus, it's mostly older guys who hang out there, and if you're just nice and polite, they tip really well. I kind of hate being a server, though. It's way too much talking to people.

July 8, 2003

Oh jeez. Today, I freaking fell asleep standing up at the register trying to put someone's food order in. Thank goodness I caught myself. I hope nobody saw me. It was only for half a second, but I almost fell over. At least the people who work here are cool . I miss working with Tosh, but I invited this guy Jared I work with and his girlfriend over to my place. They both seem pretty cool.

July 22, 2003

You're never gonna believe what happened. I did a couple lines before I went in today, and I was probably still high from last night or sleep-deprived, and I spilled HOT chili right in somebody's lap. Like the whole bowl just slid off the tray and right on their pants. I was MORTIFIED. What can you even say to a person? My face was beet red. When I clocked out, I decided I was never going back. How can I show my face in there?!?!

Jared and his girlfriend are coming over tomorrow, though. They weren't working when I did it, so I'm sure they're gonna have a good ole time making fun of me all night.

July 27, 2003

    Hard Times keeps calling me, and my heart jumps every time I see the number come up on my screen. I know I'm scheduled to come in, but I just can't get up the nerve to tell them I'm not coming back. For goodness sake, I dropped a bowl of chili on someone! Plus, I can find something else and make cash that way.

July 29, 2003

    It's kind of nice not having a job. Ha! I met this guy Calvin when I was working at Hard Times, and he actually sold me a whole 8 ball for a decent price. I've just been selling small bags of it back to Jared and cutting it with some of that baby aspirin powder. I keep some big chunks in there, though, so it isn't

WHAT'S UP?

trash. The hardest part is being disciplined not to use my whole supply. I have to stretch this out and make some money out of it until I figure out my next steps. At least I'll have enough for August rent, so that will give me some time.

August 1, 2003

Vinh mailed me this book about a girl who was doing drugs and going down the wrong path. He wrote a note inside about how he was worried about me. Boy, shut up. You weren't worried about me last year when you were out running around campus, DATING the same girl I saw you walking with. It's funny how when I accused him of it, he tried to act like I was crazy, but then the two of them actually started dating. That shit hurt. It's like when your gut tells you something is true and you know it deep down inside, but the person denies it, and then later, it becomes true. So really, I was right all along, and he never cared. Don't send me a book with a message in it acting like you care. Worry about yourself.

August 10, 2003

I had a convo with my dad today about not going back to school and taking a "gap" year, or whatever they call it. I've been so worried about it, and I'm just not prepared. Everyone kept asking, and I just kept pushing it off until finally I told him I wasn't doing it. I don't have any money or a reason to go. What am I even going for? I don't think he was upset. It seemed like he didn't really care either way, so that's good.

August 12, 2003

I've been trying to think of ways to make money. I've been hanging on, but I really don't want a regular job, and I need money ASAP. I started looking in the back of the phone book at escort services. I think you can just do the dancing part and not the other stuff. I still don't know if I could do that. I don't even like my boyfriends looking at my body naked; how the heck could I let strangers?!?! I almost called one place, but I hung up when they answered. I'll keep it in my back pocket as a last resort.

August 13, 2003

Jared and Kay came over last night. It was nuts. First, we were just chillin' in my room, listening to music and doing lines. By the middle of the night, we were all seeing shit outside my bedroom window. I swore there were these little gnome-like people and elves in the front yard. They were sort of mocking us and hanging out in the trees. We kept peeking out my window, and we all saw the same thing. It looked so real. At one point, we thought they were going to come in and try to attack us. It sounds absolutely ridiculous now, but at the time, there were 3 of us, so we felt sure that what we were seeing was real. I didn't even know coke could make you see shit like that. Maybe it was laced with something. Anyway, I'm not sure whose idea it was, but there was a large tree ax by the side door, and we decided to use it for protection. We discussed what we would do if these little elves tried to come in. Thank goodness we didn't go outside making a fool of ourselves, or, hell, go crazy and use the damn thing on each other. It's kind of funny now, but that could have ended badly!

August 14, 2003

I still haven't gone to sleep since yesterday. I don't even know how I'm writing this now. My brain is just rolling. I've been doing lines all day and tinkering around in my room. I'm kind of afraid to leave the house. I'm definitely not driving anywhere. I'm about to go take a bath. Maybe it will help me calm down a bit and relax.

August 16, 2003

You're never gonna believe this. The other night when I went to take a bath, I swear my roommate was looking at me under the door crack. It's a tiny slit between the floor and the door, and I could see his eyes staring at me! First,

I heard the creak of the wooden floor. I didn't have music or anything playing, so it was like I could hear every noise in the house. I had a few lines next to me on the table and was just chilling when I started getting sketched out. I called my mom first, then my dad, whispering that he was outside the door and I wasn't sure what to do. This went on for a while. My mom was asking all these questions, and my dad seemed just as freaked out as me. I sat there paralyzed in fear until finally, I felt like he was gone and I could grab my things and go to the room. I called my dad back today after my roommate went to work. I heard the side door close, and his car wasn't in the driveway. My dad is coming right now so I can move all my shit out and go to Calvin's house. My dad barely asked any questions, which seemed odd. Doesn't he want to know who the heck Calvin is? And more about why I'm moving? I thought when I told him some of what happened, he would want to talk to my roommate or yell at him. He had the same idea as me, though—I need to get the F out of here! He is going to bring a U-Haul so we can just throw everything in there and get out. I feel so violated. Who has the nerve to do that shit??!!? Weirdo.

August 22, 2003

Staying at Calvin's is kind of nice. I've been sleeping on his couch every night, and my dresser is just chillin' in the living room. Who the hell just lets a girl you barely know move in with you? He must be really lonely or really trusting of others. I'm thankful for him, though, because I don't know what I would have done if he hadn't let me come here. I mean, it's not a nice place. We are definitely in the projects in this little one-bedroom studio. It's small as hell, but it's just the two of us. He is a little messy, but I try to clean up when I can and sort of "pay my dues."

August 28, 2003

I'm pretty sure Calvin thinks I'm his girlfriend. He is nice and all, but I don't like him like that at all. I mean, we go to parties together and come home to watch Buffy and Charmed at 3 in the morning, but I NEVER sleep in his bed. He tried to get me to do it a couple of times, but it's just awkward. He is a big guy, though, definitely over 6 feet and probably in his 30s. I just realized I don't even know his age or his last name. Jesus. I'm always a little scared a switch is gonna flip, and he's going to make me have sex with him. I'm not paying him rent; he basically gives me coke any time I want, and any time we eat, it's on his dime. Hell, I barely see Calvin take lines. I think he just sells it because he has to. That's probably how he survives cuz he doesn't even seem to like it the same way I do. Sometimes I feel like I should just give it to him because he is taking care of me like this, but I think I would be too grossed out. For a drug dealer, he is pretty nice and chill, though. It's not like the stuff you see on TV with guns everywhere and him abusing me. He is like a big, soft teddy bear.

September 2, 2003

My face has been breaking out. I keep picking my fingers and face. I don't know how to stop. When I'm all cracked out, I feel like I need to move my body, but I don't have the energy to actually move my body, so I'm just picking at any little thing. I guess it's an anxious tick, too. I'm always a little on edge. I feel safe here, but I'm not sure I'll ever truly feel like I'm home. Ha, I didn't even feel like I was at home when I actually HAD a home.

Oh, I met this cute guy named Tommy last night while Calvin and I were at a party. We went there to sell him some snow, but they invited us in to stay. It was a little sketchy at first, but I think they were just nervous because Calvin was bringing a new girl, and they didn't know if I was a cop or something. Seriously?!? Me? A cop. Get the hell outta here. We all had a good laugh about that after doing a few lines together. Anyway, Tommy is cool. We got each other's number, so hopefully we can chill again.

September 6, 2003

We just got back from the best road trip! Calvin drives trucks for a living, apparently. How have I never seen him work or known what he does until now? I have no idea! Anyway, he took me along on this ride a few hours away. We drove through the night, and he let me hold the coke. I basically just talked to him and helped cut up lines all night. We stopped a few times for gas, but it was cool. I wonder if that's why he started doing this shit—so he could stay up and do overnight deliveries. It makes sense, especially since he doesn't seem to actually enjoy it. Well, I enjoy it! LOL. Hell, I'll take whatever he doesn't want. I'm just glad he brought me along. It basically took us 12 hours to drive there and back. Now we get some sleep.

September 9, 2003

I'm still driving on a suspended license. I had all those points back from VTech when I was going over 100 MPH trying to get home one weekend. I thought because I did the 8 hours of jail time, my record would be cleared, but then I got pulled over a couple of months ago, and they told me my license was suspended. What the hell! They gave me a warning and told me to get it checked out, or they would have to arrest me next time. For speeding?!?! That's crazy. Anyway, Calvin needs me to drive cuz he doesn't have a car, and I need a place to sleep and coke, so I guess it's all working out perfectly. There is this police officer that sits out in the neighborhood. He never really bothers anyone, but I always feel like he is watching me. Of course, I stand out like a sore thumb. Everyone around here is always hanging on the corner or being loud with their sound systems, and Calvin and I pretty much keep to ourselves. I hope he isn't watching the house for drug activity. Thankfully, Calvin never brings people to the house to buy or sell anything so we should be clear.

September 20, 2003

A guy Calvin knows asked me about doing this arranged marriage thing to help his Nigerian friend get into the country. He said he would pay me $10k, and all I have to do is get married to the guy and then act like we live together. I would have to split the money with Calvin, though, because we would use his address as the place where we live. All we would have to do is take some pictures together, put some of his clothes in drawer in the house, and answer questions if people show up asking about our marriage to see if it was legit. I'm really considering it. $10k is a lot of money, and it's not like I even have to live with this guy or have sex with him. We get married and fake that shit for a year then get divorced, and boom, $10,000! I don't know. I told him I would think about it. Calvin thinks it could be a good idea too, so we will see how it all works out.

September 23, 2003

I don't know how I'm ever going to talk to my mom again. Calvin gave me this whole 8 ball to go out and sell for him. That's almost 4 grams of coke in my hands at once. Well, I was supposed to go see my mom in Delaware for this event but started taking a few lines first because I knew I wouldn't be able to do it once I got there. Well, a few lines turned into a whole gram, and the next thing I knew, half the bag was gone. By that time, she was calling me to see how far away I was, and I kept lying and telling her I was on the way and getting closer. At one point, I knew I couldn't even drive out of the parking lot and just shut off my phone. I literally turned that shit off because every time it rang, I jumped. I don't even know what to say to her. "Oh hey, so I lied, and I was never driving your way." Then what??? Tell her I'm too coked up to drive?! Right.

She probably won't even ask me why I didn't come. That's what we do in this family — just brush all of our problems and secrets under the rug and never talk about them. And nowwwwwwww, I can't even go face Calvin cuz I'm about to finish off this bag and didn't sell any of it! I feel super guilty about that, but what did he expect? He should not have left me to my own devices. Maybe he shouldn't have been so trusting. Okay, that's wrong to blame him, but I am surprised at how clueless he seemed about me using him. It's kind of sad, really, and I shouldn't have been such a jerk. I have no clue where I'm gonna go, but I'll probably call Tommy and see if he will give me a couple dollars for what's left in this bag—or better yet, we will probably just end up snorting it together, but I know he will fill up my gas tank, so that will help.

September 26, 2003

Whoa! I have so much to tell you. Buckle up, cuz this is going to be a long one. I can't even believe what happened last night. I'm sitting here still in shock. I said I would NEVER do this, and here I am, a full-blown hypocrite. I don't regret it, even if it was one of the craziest nights of my life.

So Tommy and I have been driving around for the last couple of days, going to parties and meeting people who quickly became our best friends. Well, last night was different. We didn't go to a party. We met Rachel! Ahhhh, RACHEL!!! She lives in this cozy garage that she converted into a studio apartment, if you could even call it that. The space is bare, with only a little bit of furniture and almost no decorations or windows. It feels completely isolated from the world in the best way. Last night was different. There was no drinking or loud music, just the 3 of us. Everything felt calm, like a breath of fresh air, a new start, and a way to connect with people on a deeper level.

This girl Rachel, she reminds me so much of Tamara.

She is mesmerizing! Hell, I think she made me question my sexuality for a minute. Not in a lustful way, though. I can't really put my finger on it, but she had my full attention the whole night. She has this mysterious way about her that makes me want to be close. We became fast friends, whether she liked it or not, haha. There were a few times last night when I felt like I was in a dream. I just kind of sat back and watched her in awe. Gosh, I hope nobody saw me. It would have looked really creepy the way I was inspecting and studying her every move. I'm a little bit jealous of her. Not crazy ex-girlfriend jealous, but damn, she has this confidence that you just wanna bottle up. I could tell she doesn't give a fuck what anybody else thinks, ever. Well, at least that's what I assume, and if it's not true, then she puts on a damn good facade. No care in the world, nobody to please, no need to get permission. Just fucking freedom. I'm sure there are some assholes out there who judge her or look down on her for what she does, but I doubt she would even notice.

If I close my eyes real tight and just pause, I can imagine what it would be like to embody even just an ounce of Rachel's freedom. I would kill to be that confident, bold, daring. Even now, I can't stop thinking about her. I know it sounds like I'm obsessed, but it's not like that. I'm infatuated with her confidence and ability to say what she wants and needs. I've spent my whole damn life eager to please others. I'm always so afraid someone is going to leave me or stop calling. Rachel has figured out the damn blueprint on how to not give a fuck, and I want it!

Okay, so back to last night. I found myself sitting in a chair with my arm strapped in a belt and a needle about to plunge into my veins. I never even considered taking my drug use to this level, but at this point, I'm pretty sure there is no turning back.

Rachel told me to sit in the chair. I barely hesitated before I sat down and gripped the arm of the chair with both hands, knuckles white with fear, excitement, and anticipation all at the same time. I asked how to do it myself, but she reassured me that she would take care of all the details. I just had to sit there and relax. I don't know why, but I had this air of confidence when she gushed about the fact I had plump, clean veins. She couldn't wait to stick me with that needle. Even Rachel seemed a bit giddy, but she made sure to take care of me every step of the way. I could tell she had been doing this for a while. Each step was deliberate and intentional. She used the syringe and soaked up some water from a bottle cap. She crouched down beside me with one knee on the floor and the other sitting upright to hold her tools. It was as if she were my mother, taking care of a bloody knee after falling off my bike. That sounds ridiculous, but seriously, she was so focused and caring, reassuring me at every moment. After she grabbed a spoon and a bump of cocaine, she squirted the water methodically onto

woah!

the spoon and gently used the plunger from the syringe to swirl it around so that the mixture became a cloudy white color. She used this cotton ball to absorb the liquid before drawing it into the needle. Nobody said why, but I think it's so you don't inject weird shit into your body that isn't supposed to be there. That seems a little ironic, huh? Anyway, my heart was starting to beat out of my chest. You would think I was scared or worried about dying, but none of that even crossed my mind. I was ready. There was a certain type of freedom that came with accepting my fate, regardless of the outcome. I could hardly wait to feel that rush! I remember the first time I snorted cocaine in the high school bathroom, and I was pretty sure this was going to blow that experience right out of the water. Well, it did not disappoint!

Rachel turned the syringe upside down and flicked it with her finger once before getting the air pockets out of the needle. She placed the syringe sideways in her mouth and gripped it between her teeth for easy access. She tied my arm off with one of those long brown rubber bands you see at the blood bank. It was in a half tie so she could remove it quickly when the time came. It pinched a little when she put it on, but the feeling was familiar, and I liked that.

I squeezed my hand into a fist so she could find my biggest vein. When she pulled back the plunger, you could see a little bit of my blood enter the clear liquid vial. She slowly pushed the sweet, sweet medicine into my veins before reminding me to open my fist as she took the tie off my arm. I can remember that huge rush of blood pumping up the left side of my body, down the right, and back up again. My whole body was tingling, and the rush attacked me methodically, following my veins through every part, up my arm, across my chest, then down my legs. I couldn't move; I felt quite literally paralyzed. I didn't know if I was going to piss on myself or throw up, but it was the most free I've ever felt in my life. The drip in the back of my throat was way worse than snorting coke, but worth every second.

I think it took me a few minutes before I could even speak! I took a huge exhale and opened my eyes. They were all standing around me waiting for this moment. A huge smile shot across Rachel's face. "It's amazing, isn't it?"

FEELING CUTE

she said. She probably had no idea what she had just done, but Rachel helped me find the cure to most of my problems. I feel bad now for judging people who shoot up. Shit, if I had known how good it was, I probably would have tried it sooner.

That night we started out as complete strangers, and now they are all part of one of the most significant nights of my life. I can't believe we ventured out to the corner store. Thank God nobody noticed how messed up we were. Shit, I could have dropped dead, and nobody would have known what to do or who to call.

Alright, well, gotta go. Talk later!

September 30, 2003

This is the story of Mr. Fox. This is not a Dr. Seuss rhyme, I promise. He sounds like a made-up character, and to be honest, I couldn't even tell you one thing about him, except that he knows Tommy, lives an extravagant life, and loves doing lines of crystal. Snorting it is definitely different than shooting it, but still fun as hell. We were all just dancing in Mr. Fox's apartment, tweaking out to The Crystal Method, until I got super paranoid. I went outside to call my dad and leave, but I seriously had no idea where I was. I was trying to find street signs, but I could barely read them, and then I was scared of being out there alone. I went and found my car and just hid out there for the night. I couldn't sleep until the sun came out. I must have passed out after that because I don't even really remember anything else from the night.

October 3, 2003

Rachel and I linked up today. We are going to go to Tommy's friend's house. I didn't tell them, but I was able to get needles on my own yesterday. I don't think they would judge me or anything, but I also don't want them to know I've been shooting up basically every day since we met. Rachel would probably feel bad for introducing me to it. I was using the same needle from that first night but have seen enough movies to know that's not safe. I'm not trying to get sick from an infection and die. I'm also afraid the tiny metal is going to break off and get stuck in my arm. How would I even explain that to anyone? You can't go to the hospital because a needle is stuck in your arm. That's just ridiculous.

I went to a pharmacy and lied, saying I needed the needles for my grandma to take her diabetes medication. They didn't even flinch when I asked for the package of 10cc needles. I guess my face has cleared up enough, and I'm wearing long sleeves so you don't see any needle pokes or the bandaid on my veins. Well, now I have a nice fresh bag of needles. Can't wait to use them tonight! Tommy said his friend knows how to make meth, too. I don't know if they make it in their house, but I assume it's a bunch of chemicals mixed together. I don't know how these people make it and sell it. I feel like I would just be high all day and too afraid to leave the house.

October 7, 2003

I'm still not sure if these are all the same things or just different variations or kinds of methamphetamine. It sounds like a lab experiment. Technically, I guess it is. People make the shit in bathtubs for goodness sake.

Meth	Girl	Ice
CRYSTAL (my fav!)	Crank	Glass
Tina	Speed	

October 8, 2003

Yesterday was stranger than usual. I met Tyler and Jeremy at a party the other night. I don't even remember exchanging numbers with them, but they were cool, so I guess I figured they had a connect and I could link up with them in the future. Jeremy was driving us around in this black pickup truck. I would have driven myself, but my license is STILL suspended, and I'm not trying to get another warrant for my arrest. Plus, I was high as a kite already. I had no idea where we were even going. I was just along for the ride at this point.

The guys got in the front while I sat in the back of the cab. I feel like I've reached a new level of drug use, like I've unlocked the code. Rachel told me about speedballing, where you take turns doing coke and then meth. It all seems to hit you like a stack of bricks—no lead up, no waiting, just BAM. You feel like you're floating in the sky, way above any problem you could imagine. You don't even care what is going on around you, well, until you start coming down, of course. After you get that first high, you're always trying to chase the weightless feeling. It's a never-ending process, but I wouldn't trade it for the world.

I must have been pretty high, because I was starting to get paranoid, past the point of floating for sure. The guys were talking up front as I sat quietly in the back. I was definitely in my head. I thought everything they were talking about was in code and they were going to kill me. I had convinced myself they were planning to rape me and how they would dispose of my body. Maybe that sounds arrogant cuz I look like shit right now. I was lucky they were even driving around with me. I have no money or anything to offer at this point other than some company.

It seemed like we were driving forever, and I had lost all sense of time. We were definitely not in DC anymore. There were only two lanes of traffic, and the license plates looked different. I was so damn confused. The license plates were pretty, like a sunset scene from a desert. "Holy shit," I thought. "Are we in Arizona?" It sounds absurd now.

There is no way we could have driven across the country in the amount of time we were driving. I couldn't make sense of it. The paranoia really started getting to me.

At one point, I was scanning the car for an exit. We were on the highway, but I thought if I had to, I could jump out of the car and roll myself to safety, and then I would only have minor injuries. What an idiot. I literally have no money, nobody to call, and am clueless about my location. Needless to say, I stayed put in the car and lived to tell about it.

October 10, 2003

Damn, I'm getting desperate. I spent today driving around, sleeping in the car, and trying to find change under the seats to buy food off the dollar menu. It's been really rainy, and I didn't even have clean water in the car. My ass decided it was a good idea to collect rainwater in my spoon to mix the coke in the syringe. I felt like MacGyver and a badass coming up with that idea. Needless to say, it worked, and the high was unbelievable. I'm still tweaking from it, and bonus points because I didn't care about eating much after that. I always try to look back and think about what I was doing when I was high. Soooo much time passes, but I barely do anything at all. Just a lot of roaming around, driving to new spots, messing with stuff in the car, or picking my damn fingers. I have to stop doing that because it's getting embarrassing, but I can't help it. I need something to use up the energy, and I can't exactly go run a mile.

October 12, 2003

Tommy introduced me to a new group of his friends today. We went over to their townhouse and stayed a while. None of them were doing drugs in the open, but I felt like everyone was doing it in secret or talking about it. I was super sketched out. Usually, we go to parties, and everyone just has it lying around or pulls the bags out, cuts it up, and snorts it together right there. It seemed like they were definitely hiding something. I mean, I was a stranger to them, so I get it now.

First, I thought they were talking shit about me and were going to steal my drugs or my car, but then I calmed myself down and decided the girls looked too friendly and there were more of us than guys. THEN I realized that wasn't it. They were going to try to help me or save me! In my mind, I thought they probably called my parents and arranged some intervention. So my dumbass flushed everything I had down their toilet and left. It was dark now, and I couldn't drive because I had a headlight out, so I went to the mall parking lot and slept there until the morning. I called my dad, and he came and found me and let me follow him back to his place for the day. I had to hide the needle in the sole of my shoe and the metal spoon in my purse. My dad didn't ask any questions. So bizarre. The only sense I can make of it is from when he first gave me a beeper and then a cell phone when I was 14. I remember he told me he would pay for it as long as when he called me, I always called him back immediately. He also said that if I was ever in a bad situation, like if friends were drinking and I couldn't get a safe ride home, then I had to promise to call him. While I'm clearly not following all of those rules, I guess he knows that if I call, I'm probably in trouble, and if he started asking a bunch of questions, I would stop calling.

I'm not sure why I didn't trash my spoon and needles too, but I was afraid if I threw them out the window, the police could pull DNA off them or something and come find me. It's ridiculous, but my brain loves to play crazy tricks on me when I'm messed up and clearly paranoid to the tenth degree. It is nice to get a shower and some rest and real food. I wonder what Tommy thinks! I'm actually surprised he hasn't called me yet to see where I went.

October 19, 2003

Jeeeeez. I hardly remember last night. I haven't even gone to sleep yet. It feels like the longest day ever. I'm still here at this guy Floyd's house. There are random people all over the place. Some passed out, and others were still tweaking about. They live in this chill townhouse, and his uncle Buzzy lives a couple of doors down, so we were going back and forth between the houses. Floyd has two other roommates, but they are into some other shit, like Special K. I don't know what that is, but they said it's some type of tranquilizer. That shit sounds scary. Who wants to be basically paralyzed around a bunch of strangers? No, thank you. There were lines of meth everywhere, though, and everyone was really generous. Buzzy's wife doesn't mess with that shit, but she was still cool hanging out with everyone and drinking. I even tried smoking crystal out of foil. It wasn't bad, but not my cup of tea. The high was real quick and then gone. I feel like I would just be puffing all day. The girl Jen said it's called "chasing the dragon" because you constantly want to feel that first rush. Hell, if that's the case, I've been chasing the dragon trying to find my first high from that needle in Rache's place.

October 20, 2003

Welp, I'm still here. I think they have adopted me, LOL. Okay, not really, but I've become the lady of the house around here. I still haven't slept since I got here on Floyd's birthday, but I started cleaning up the aftermath of the party. I even went to the grocery store and got like $300 worth of groceries. Honestly, I know there isn't any money in there, but I was able to write a check, and they accepted it, so I'll have to deal with that later. I'm going to make everyone a big breakfast later once we all get hungry. It's been a few days since anybody has eaten, so once everything wears off, we are going to be ravenous. It feels nice to take care of some people, and I'm glad they aren't rushing me out of here. Floyd's room is cozy. It's small, but he has a comfortable mattress on the floor and a TV in there. It's private, so we can chill alone when there are lots of people in the house. Buzzy has been letting us hang over there too in the basement. They have kids, so we always hang out in the shop down in the basement.

October 27, 2003

Dammit. I tried to start my car this morning to grab more food, and it just wouldn't turn over. Literally just dead. Floyd is gonna have Buzzy look at it later. I'm glad I grabbed a bunch of my stuff from Calvin's before abandoning that place. I've been here for like a week and definitely need to freshen up. My car is packed with clothes, pictures, books, and random things I've saved from Tech. I've started bringing some of my clothes and stuff inside the house because it's really a pain to keep going out there every time I need a brush for my hair or get a shower. Oh, they have a tub here too, but it's upstairs at Buzzy's house where the kids' rooms are!! The kids are so nice. I try not to look high around them, though. I think that's weird. They have to wonder why all these people are in their house all the time and they can't go in the basement, right??? I can't wait until later when I can snort a few lines, smoke a cigarette, and just chill in the tub alone without fear of some creep staring at me.

November 3, 2003

Buzzy has been teaching me about the different types of meth. You can tell if it's good shit based on how it looks. I guess the stuff that literally looks like glass or ice is pretty clean and high-quality. You also see some stuff that looks more powdery with a yellowish tint. That stuff is usually harder and doesn't crush up as nicely. I'm thinking it must be cut with a different type of chemical. Either way, the shit burns like hell going up your nose. I definitely prefer shooting it, but Buzzy isn't really a fan and definitely doesn't want us doing it in his house. I guess he's afraid one of us is gonna OD, and then how do you explain that to the cops?!

November 11, 2003

I don't even know how she found me! I hadn't talked to my mom in a couple of months when I just disappeared off the face of the earth. I almost left Floyd's, though. I can't believe they all came up here. It still feels like a dream. I'm not 100% sure it really even happened at this point. We did so much meth over the last 3 days, I don't even think I've

slept or eaten in about 72 hours. I was seriously tweaking.
I never even told her what city I was in, and I don't
have his address, so how the hell did she get it??? Well, it
wasn't just her; it was all of my uncles, too. That was super
intimidating. It definitely took me off guard. They were
pleading with me, begging me to come home with them. My
head was spinning. I couldn't even process what the heck
they were saying to me. Leave? And go where? Why would
I go home? What is even there for me? At the same time, I
know I'm not happy doing this, but it just feels like there is
no other option. I literally don't care what happens to me.
Is that weird? It's like I've given up, or maybe just accepted
the fact I'm not meant for happiness. Snorting lines, staying
up all night, and doing weird shit has become my life now. I
don't even have a place to live. I've just sort of moved into
Floyd's house, and until he kicks me out, I guess I'm staying
here. I've stayed in the car a couple of days before, but
that's way too sketchy. This is definitely more comfortable
here, plus, Floyd and I have this *thing* going on now. We've
been attached at the hip since we met on his birthday.

One of my uncles pulled me to the side and was pretty
convincing. I don't even know what he was saying, but I
remember feeling like he understood what was going on
with me. He told me how he had gone down this path before
and had wished someone stopped him, so that's what they
were trying to do last night. I just couldn't give it up. I was
so close to saying, "Okay, I'll leave," but the words wouldn't

come out of my mouth, and what would Floyd think? I can't just leave. I'm not sure how long we were all outside with them trying to convince me, but it was exhausting. After a whole bunch of drama and them trying to come inside and begging me to come back out, I went back inside and just went to sleep for what felt like an eternity. I do kinda feel bad that they had to leave, but how the hell was I just gonna pack up my stuff and go home? That's weird. So here I am. I need a shower. My eyes are all black, and I'm pretty sure if I don't eat soon, I'm going to die from starvation.

November 22, 2003

We have been on a roll lately! I've gotten so skinny, which is nice, but I've been getting black circles under my eyes and really picking my fingers a lot. I have to stop that shit! I can barely keep track of time anymore. I only know it's time to sleep or eat when my eyes are burning and dry and my ribs feel completely sunken into my body. I guess this is love. <3

December 18, 2003

Jesus, this journal is like a damn folder of evidence at this point, but I don't even care. You're like the best friend I never knew I needed, especially during this time of insane experiences. I don't think anyone would have ever thought this would be my life. Writing everything in here has been good for my soul, and maybe my conscience at some points, too.

Last time I saw my dad, he gave me a couple of family heirloom things. One was a ruby ring from my great-grandmother and a check from my grandmother for Christmas. I've definitely been in need of some cash, so it was right on time. I did some fucked-up shit, though, because I was so desperate. I really don't think anyone will notice, but I do regret it a little bit. I just keep thinking I'll probably be dead before anyone finds out about all this bad stuff I've done. My grandma wrote the check out for $50, and I made it into $80. The numbers were easy, but I had to write in cursive to change the words, too. I really took my time doing it, and apparently, it worked, cuz they gave me the 80 bucks!

December 28, 2003

Ughhhhh, I just keep doing bad stuff. I feel kind of awful, but what are my options? I shouldn't even write this in here. If anyone ever finds this journal, I'm screwed, but I had to tell someone. I have zero dollars to my name at this point. I've used every penny left in my bank account and already pawned anything of value I had—including my own laptop from college and that ruby ring from my grandma :(

I felt awful for that one, but what was I gonna do with

it? I needed the money to survive at this point.

Since it's confession time, I might as well tell you. One of Floyd's roommates, Kirk, had his book bag on the couch. For some reason, nobody was home except for me, and I was being nosy. He had a laptop and charging cord in there. I thought about it for a while, and then on a bit of a whim, I snatched it up and hid it in my car. Later, I took it to the pawn shop and got a couple hundred bucks for it. He was so upset, and everyone was looking for it and trying to come up with ideas about where it could be. We had a party the night before and half of them were high off Ketamine so they didn't remember either. The whole time I'm sitting there knowing I freaking stole it but pretending to look all around the house and come up with ideas. He is seriously the nicest guy, and I could never admit what I did. They didn't suspect me at all. This is going to haunt me forever. It would be one thing to steal from a store, but I know this guy, and he has done NOTHING wrong to me. I don't know what got into me. I just wasn't thinking, I guess, or maybe I've gone too far this time.

POWER OF CHOICE

January 1, 2004

I almost left.

He hit me last night. He literally smacked me across the face. Stupid jerk!

I must have had the most shocked look on my face, but of course, he didn't say anything, and neither did I...

I was so excited to finally get out of the house. It feels like we have just been home for weeks, stuck in that tiny bedroom or walking down the road to Buzzy's. We were going to a New Year's Eve party. It was this dark, seemingly abandoned house, but people did actually live there because the heat was on, there was running water, and a few random pieces of furniture. Everyone was partying and having a good night. I barely met anyone because Floyd and I were just tied at the hip and all fucked up. Before we went to bed (or rather crashed on the floor), we went into the bathroom for a little privacy. Nobody else was tying off, and we didn't want people staring. We shot up before he put me on top of the sink to...you know. Anyway, I must have said something smart or silly after he finished. I know I wasn't trying to be rude or mean. I was just trying to lighten the mood since we just had sex in a bathroom at some random person's house. I felt a little awkward and gross. Then, here he goes and hauls off and smacks me clear across the face. As if I wasn't already embarrassed enough, my face turned beet red, and I froze in a panic. He had never put his hands on me before. I didn't even react other than staring at him in silence. There was no gasp, no crying, and I certainly didn't try to find out why the hell he did it. We both zipped up our pants, collected ourselves, and left the bathroom to find a place to lie down.

This morning is when the anger kicked in. I was pissed. I refuse to turn into my mom. I brought up the incident from the night before with him and started to instigate a fight. Deep down I was hoping he would just apologize so we could move on. But no, he doubled down and blamed ME for what happened. So today, after he was yelling and screaming and blaming me for ruining his entire night, I decided I was going to leave.

I tried to grab what little was left of my things and went out to my car, then I quickly realized the battery was dead and I wouldn't be going anywhere. At this point, my pride was hurt, and there was no way I was returning to the house. And of course, there were several freaking inches of snow, and it was freezing outside. I put on as many layers of clothes as possible and just started walking. I literally had no idea where I was going, but he had to know he couldn't control me like that. I can't just let somebody hit me, especially for no good reason. It didn't take too long before I came up to a gas station. I was standing outside forever, with no clue what to do. I had a few cigarettes on me, so that kept me busy for a while, but it started getting darker and colder. I considered calling someone to come pick me up. Maybe my mom? My dad? I definitely couldn't call my mom. She would have way too many questions, and how the hell is she gonna come down here and pick me up? That just seems ridiculous. I'm hours away from her. Then I realized my dad is in freaking Florida, so he can't save me. I must have looked desperate because a man finally asked me if I needed a ride or wanted to call somebody. He seemed so nice, but when he asked me those questions, it all kind of hit me at once. I have NOBODY I can call and nowhere he can drive me. What the hell am I waiting here for? No miracle is going to happen standing out there freezing my ass off. I was running away from Floyd, but where was I gonna go?

Sooooo here I am, writing in this damn journal back at the house. Walking back inside was the worst. I definitely tucked my tail between my legs and just quietly came in the door. He didn't even say anything to me. He was probably feeling himself cuz he knew I couldn't go anywhere. It's not like I'm gonna leave my car here forever. Shit, he probably didn't even care that I left.

Now I'm here, pissed off, watching Floyd tinker with his stupid samurai sword and listening to weird-ass music.

January 18, 2004

I don't know what it is, but I can't even finish a whole cigarette anymore. A few puffs, and I gotta put it out. I was smoking like half a pack to a full pack a day, and now I can hardly smoke two cigarettes over an entire day. Maybe my body is just rejecting it for some reason. I've been more hungry lately, too. It's like I'm a lightweight. One of the girls was joking and said I was probably pregnant. Can you imagine?!! That would just be absurd at this point.

February 17, 2004

Once again, you are NOT going to believe this. It's straight out of a movie at this point. On a whim, Katie and I went to get a pregnancy test since I've been having weird cravings and feeling tired all the time. I thought it was a stupid idea. Ummmm, well, that shit had TWO PINK LINES!!! I had to read the directions again because, honestly, I was in shock. We didn't even have to wait the five minutes. As soon as I peed, it started to change colors. I'm glad now that I've been smoking less. Now I'm done for good. I guess I won't be hanging in the basement with everyone anymore, either. All that shit is done. No more cigarettes, no alcohol, no coke, and definitely no meth! Floyd seemed pretty shocked with the news too, but we are trying to figure out how all of this would work. I'm so excited. I can't believe I'm going to be a mom. I definitely was NOT expecting this.

February 20, 2004

We have been sleeping at Buzzy's house in a room upstairs. I don't know what is with Floyd and his roommates. I think he didn't pay them, or maybe they didn't want me staying there, but they kicked him out. We gotta find something else long-term cuz we can't just mooch off his uncle. Their little daughter Alice is so sweet, though. She is only 6 years old and just the cutest little thing. When everyone is partying, I've been making sure she has dinner, helping her fold her clothes, and playing games with her.

February 27, 2004

We told Floyd's mom that we're pregnant. She seemed excited. She even asked us to move in with her so she could help us. I think that would be the best idea for us, but Floyd isn't so sure. He and Buzzy work together, and it's hard enough for him to wake up on time as it is. It would be even harder if we didn't live with them. I mean, he has a point. I would like to get out of this drug house, though. I've been thinking of how we could have the baby in this space with us right now, and it would be tight. We are already sleeping on a mattress on the floor. I doubt we could fit a bassinet or anything. I just want a space that will be safe for all of us.

March 3, 2004

Floyd had one of his little fits of rage again last night and tore my shit up. It brought me to tears. He knows I don't have much left, and he took the things he knows I care the most about and destroyed them!!! My Virginia Tech shirt was ripped to shreds, my grandmother's pearl necklace torn apart and all of my best-mixed CD's busted in half. All I can think of is what he would have done if all the baby's stuff was here. Would he still have lost his temper? I really can't understand why he wants to hurt me so badly. And thank God he didn't touch me. I know I don't LOOK pregnant yet, but jeez, I'm caring for a life inside of me. I can't stay with him here and put the baby at risk, too.

March 5, 2004

I called my mom today. I finally told her I was pregnant. Actually, first I made sure she was sitting down. Then I said, "Well, I made it longer than you. I waited until I was 19 to get pregnant." She didn't think it was as funny as I did. I think she was silent for a really long time. She sounded like she wanted to be excited for me but didn't know what to say. She asked me if I was keeping the baby. I thought that was a weird question because what else was I going to do? Of course I'm keeping the baby. I never even questioned another option. I felt a bit of relief after telling her. She wants us to come visit her. I'm not sure how we could do that just yet. I guess I could get Buzzy to check out my car and see if he could fix it. Floyd's mom knows a mechanic, too. Hopefully, they can get it running, and get us some gas to get there and we can go visit. My mom has never even officially met Floyd, so it would be good for her to get to know the father of my child.

♡ ♡ ♡ Baby ♡ ♡ ♡

March 19, 2004

That did not go as planned! We made it to Delaware last night, and it was wild. I stood there in the hallway, eye to eye with my mother in what felt like a Western standoff. I guess now that I'm going to be a mom, I have a little extra spunk. It was an act of rebellion talking to her the way I did. This past year has really changed me. I was finally ready to fight—not physically, but my body was screaming from the inside. I rarely speak up for myself, but I just can't keep quiet anymore.

My mom is staying with my grandmother right now, so both of them were there. When I pictured coming here, I really made this visual in my head that I would be in a safe place and they could take care of me. Deep down inside, I was hoping they would scoop me up, give me a huge hug, feed me homemade meals, and make me lie down to take a rest as they wrapped me in warm blankets. I know it sounds ridiculous, but I just needed someone to care.

But of course, it was nothing like that. It all came to a head when my mom started getting in Floyd's face and accusing him of being disrespectful. She actually asked him to leave the house. Matter of fact, when he refused, she LITERALLY kicked him out—like pushed and shoved him out the door—and locked it. I was livid. He was definitely being disrespectful, but why would she do that? Did she even care what I thought? She didn't even consider how he would get home or what was going to happen to me now that she had done this to him. I don't know how I convinced her to let him back in the house. He was instigating her the whole time and getting super loud. My grandmother was going to call the police. I think after I threatened to leave if they made him leave, they reconsidered and let us both stay. It was NOT comfortable, to say the least. I was screaming. My mom was screaming, and Floyd was a mess. At one point, I was between the two of them, standing in front of Floyd, protecting him from my mom. I just really wanted it to stop. I can't deal with this kind of stress while I'm pregnant. My car is acting up again, so I think Floyd's mom is going to pick us both up tomorrow. I hope Floyd lets us stay with her at her house. I know I would feel better, and I'm sure she can make him get to work on time.

March 21, 2004

What am I doing? I don't know if I'm happy or if I should cry. We were driving back to Virginia when Floyd's mom could see how upset I was with the whole situation. I was really confused, and my mom was begging me to stay with her before we left. We were only 30 minutes into the drive when I spoke up and told her we needed to turn around. I don't know what got into me, but I knew I needed to go back. It felt like a really big moment, and I was scared to say anything, but it's not just about me anymore. I knew Floyd wasn't going to be able to come stay with me, but we can figure that out later. I need a safe place for the baby, and this is the best shot we have right now. Plus, I don't want to be near all those drugs and people coming in and out. Floyd hardly sees me anyway now that I'm not in the mix. He is either working or hanging out in the basement. We can still talk, and I'll come visit once my car stuff is all settled.

I just keep repeating these lyrics in my head to stay on the right path:

"We'll never part, sickness and health.

You are my heart.

I love you more than I love myself."

(Can-I-Bus)

April 5, 2004

My mom keeps trying to get me to go to these drug treatment centers where you literally check yourself in. I thought about it, but I don't think I need it. Seeing the people there is depressing, and I'm not trying to be pregnant and locked up. Some of them are really expensive too. I've already got student loan debt, and I'm not trying to add more.

Oh, and apparently that police officer who used to sit outside Calvin's house...well, my mom has his number. I guess at some point when she came to Virginia with my uncles she was looking for me and went to that neighborhood and he recognized me. She called him recently to let him know I was home safe and pregnant now. He looked up my info, and apparently, there is still a warrant out for my arrest because of all the times I was caught driving on a suspended license and missed court dates. How would I have even known? I didn't even have a solid address they could have sent the notice to. He said we could pick a day and drive down to Virginia, and he would meet us at the station to help take care of everything. Then at least I don't have to get booked and locked in a cell.

That's pretty cool of him, and I guess it's good for me to get everything taken care of so I can drive my car again when the baby is born.

May 16, 2004

I've been obsessed with donuts! I had six in one day just last week. I don't have any weird cravings, but I can eat donuts all day. Oh, and McDonalds—a Big Mac, salty fries, and ice-cold sweet tea. This baby LOVES TO EAT!! I guess now that I'm not curbing my appetite with these drugs, my body is trying to stock up.

Floyd and I have been emailing every now and then. He is trying to work a lot to save up money for the baby. He said he is going to send me some in a few weeks. I might go visit him when I take care of the court situation.

May 22, 2004

I've been acting like everything is okay, and I guess for the most part it is, but I still feel like something is missing. I have all this responsibility now and a freaking baby, but I'm still lost. My dumb ass put a belt around my arm the other day and squeezed my fist tight before poking a pen on my inner arm. I released the belt and laid back as if the "medicine" was rushing up the left side of my body. I felt disgusted afterward. It wasn't real, but the fact I would even pretend when I have a baby inside of me is stupid. Maybe I do need help, but I just can't bring myself to do it. That's the closest I've had to a craving, and I sure as hell wouldn't go out here and find any REAL drugs. That's just insane. I took my little black book with everyone's numbers the other day and threw it out. Just threw it in the garbage. There is literally no reason why I would need any of those numbers or addresses, or hell, any of the memories ever again. Bye-bye old life!

20 YEARS OLD

June 11, 2004

Going to the ultrasound tomorrow to find out if we are having a boy or a girl, so that is exciting!!! I'll report back tomorrow with the good news. :)

June 12, 2004

What a weekend. Now that the car situation is fixed, I drove down to stay with Floyd's mom and get an ultrasound. Floyd was supposed to come, but he was being an ass and fighting with his mom, so she just took me by herself. She got us a hotel room for the night so we could spend time together, but we just ended up arguing. I was crying out for him to care about everything that was going on, and he just seemed mad. I guess he feels like I abandoned him, but I feel like HE is the one abandoning us. I don't know what I said to make him mad, but at one point, he flicked his lit cigarette into my suitcase. Thank God it didn't light on fire. We were in a hotel room, for goodness sake. He has been doing all kinds of little stuff to push me away. At his mom's house, he threw a full soda can at my face. It nicked the corner of my eye, and it started bleeding. I was able to cover it up long enough and acted like I opened the corner of the car door on myself. When I came back home, I'm not even sure my mom believed that one, but I made sure to visualize it in my head. It's so real to me now that it's the only way I can picture it. Heck, now I'm starting to question if he really did throw it at me or if it truly was the car door, LOL. I really hate lying, but I feel like it's the only way to protect him right now...

July 7, 2004

I got a marketing job. It sounds way more glamorous than it actually is, but it pays decently, and my mom works there too. It helps that we can work the same schedule, and she just drives both of us. My car situation is finally fixed, but to get insurance with all of my past issues is like $500 a month, and that's just stupid. I'm making more money, but not THAT much, especially since I'm trying to save up for the baby.

Floyd hasn't been returning any of my calls or emails. Some days I sit there at work and write him these long emails about everything that has been going on, and he just ignores them. His phone barely ever works and is never turned on. I used to try to call his mom and Buzzy, but I was starting to feel crazy. It's like I'm screaming on the inside. I just want to grab and shake him. How can he not care about any of this? Me? HIS BABY? He doesn't even know we are having a girl. Does he even care? Probably not. Am I supposed to move on? It certainly doesn't seem like he is trying to get himself together and move up here closer to us. I'm definitely not moving back there for a long time. I'm just sad. This sucks.

July 17, 2004

I don't think I told you, but my dad moved back to Delaware too. Anyway, I didn't have the heart to tell him that I was pregnant. I feel like he will be disappointed or sad for me. I'm still small but clearly pregnant. I have to wear maternity clothes, for goodness sake. Today he took me on my grandfather's boat, and I didn't even wear a bathing suit. I had these khaki pants with an elastic band and this white flowy top. There is NO WAY he didn't notice, but neither of us said a word. What is there to say, really? Eventually I guess he will find out, LOL.

July 23, 2004

I've been going to this teen girls' group. My mom had me talk to her therapist a few weeks ago, and she recommended this other counselor who is hosting a group for teen girls in abusive relationships. I never really thought of it that way before, but I guess I've always been in and out of abusive relationships. That word just seems harsh. She had us write down this list of all the traits of our partner, then all the ideal traits we would like in a partner, and then a list of our traits. It was crazy to see the contrast between Floyd and what I wanted. It was eye-opening. It's nice to have other girls my age who have been through something similar to me.

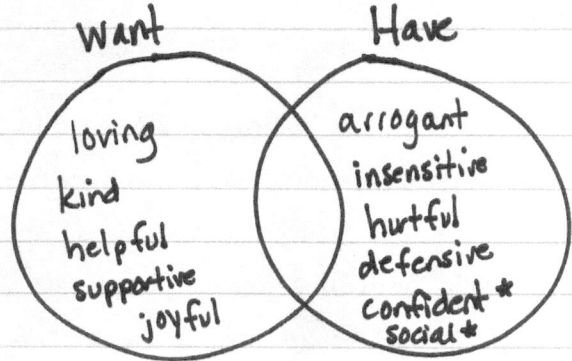

August 5, 2004

I've tried to stop emailing Floyd altogether. What's the point?

Actually, I started talking to a guy on MySpace. He is pretty cool but lives down in Dover. He is in the Air Force. I think the Air Force guys have a bad reputation, but he seems like a nice guy. We talk almost every day, and I get excited when he messages me back. I did tell him I was like seven months pregnant, but he didn't seem to mind. I think that is pretty cool, but it does make me wonder why in the heck he would want to date a pregnant girl. I'm going to drive down and meet him for lunch next week. We will see how it goes.

August 19, 2004

I've been doing so well saving money and really getting a nice little nest egg before the baby comes. She is due the first week in October, and I've been going to a birth center so I can have her naturally. I don't want to be hooked up to any IVs or anything that could trigger me to want to go back to that old life.

I was so pissed the other day. On top of wearing my favorite jeans and RIPPING THEM, my mom needed new tires and basically forced me to pay for them. I get that we are driving in your car and you aren't making me pay rent or anything, but I just don't like how she assumed I should pay for them like it was my duty. When she was wearing my pants, she bent over, and they ripped right up the middle. She just laughed and thought it was funny. It's already bad enough I work with all of these young, cute girls who get to wear regular clothes, and I'm over here like a whale about to pop. Now I can't even wear my cute jeans once I can fit back into them. I know it's not the end of the world, but it's just another slap in the face. You would think since she had me when she was only 18, she would understand what it's like and be a LITTLE bit more considerate, but no, she just shoves it in my face!

September 20, 2004

I'm getting so big. I'm almost ready to pop. At this point, I'm sick of being pregnant. It's kind of lonely, though. I can't wait until she gets here. I can't believe I'm going to be a freaking mom. I have no idea how I'm going to do all of this, but I'm really not scared. It feels like a fresh start, a way to do something new and great. I'm counting down the days.

October 3, 2004

She's here!!!! She is the most beautiful, precious thing I've ever seen in my life. My mom was in the room with me holding my legs, and as soon as she came out, I got to put her right on my chest. I've never been so in love in my life. It was like the gaping hole inside of me was instantly filled. She is the best baby, too. It's been really hard nursing, and we've had to keep her in the sunlight because she has been getting jaundice, but she isn't hard at all. I love snuggling with her on my chest. It's the best feeling.

I told "Air Force boy" and he is going to come visit. I didn't even try to tell Floyd. His mom and sisters know. I think they are going to come up and visit with his grandmother. I'm really happy they didn't abandon us and are trying to stay involved. I've pretty much given up on him, but I'm glad baby Bri will have them to rely on.

MY LITTLE ANGEL

October 5, 2004

It's only been a couple of days, and my grandmother has not stopped nagging me. She keeps telling me I'm sleeping too much and need to get my laundry done. I guess she doesn't like the baby bottles out all the time, either. Can't she tell I'm trying my best here? I JUST had a baby and am trying to figure out how to nurse her and squeeze in a few hours of sleep each night. I know my family is trying to help, but it would be nice to have a little bit more support right now.

October 10, 2004

It's only been a little over a week, and your girl is back in her regular jeans!! Granted, I had to squeeze into those things, but I did it LOL. I cannot stand wearing maternity clothes for one more second. I felt like a big cow, and now I'm finally starting to get a little confidence back. Plus, if I'm going to be out here dating again, I want to look good—not like a new mom.

October 22, 2004

I've been grieving my childhood a lot lately—the one I never had. I guess that's what you would call it: grief. I cry a lot, and I'm angry and just plain sad about it all. I can't place my finger on it, but it feels like I was robbed of something. Maybe the fun of it or being carefree? It just seems like I've been stressed my whole life, and maybe something is wrong with me. Now when I look back, I wonder if I started using drugs to take away the pain or maybe just as a way to deal with everything. I'm not sure it actually worked, but I guess it allowed me not to feel all of these emotions. Now that I'm clean, it's like they are all hitting me at once, and it's overwhelming.

I just can't wait to be the mom I always needed for my little girl. I feel so, so grateful that I'm one of the lucky ones that made it out. I know a lot of people can't stop drugs the way I did. They get pregnant and keep using, or they wait until they have the baby and then start back up again. I am NOT doing that. I can't do that. It's not about me anymore. I have to take care of her. She saved my LIFE!!! If it weren't for her, I'm pretty sure I would be dead in a ditch by now. I don't think my family understands that. We still haven't talked about ANY of this since I got home. I find it strange, but also a bit relieving. I don't really want to talk about it with them, but I'm surprised they aren't more curious. They have no idea what goes on in this head of mine. I feel tormented every day by how I feel, but this baby has finally given me true hope that I deserve to be alive and I can make changes for the future.

October 29, 2004

I went to visit Floyd's family with the baby. I finally feel like a stable adult. I wasn't even worried about seeing him. I have this little bit of confidence and sureness about myself and my life. I actually kind of feel sorry for him. Sorry that he didn't get to have the change I did with this pregnancy. Sorry that he is still stuck in this loop of nothingness. The visit was nice. I was feeling pretty overwhelmed at one point, though, and said the baby needed to nurse even though I knew she wasn't hungry. I just needed some time alone by ourselves. There were too many people touching her, pulling her from me, and all the noise. I felt like I was spinning in circles. I took her into one of the rooms in private, and we just fell asleep together. Floyd did end up coming over and got to hold her and see her. He cried a little bit, like a single tear. It was nice to see some emotion from him, but I don't expect much more. He said he wants to call more and is living with his mom now and getting a new phone. It all sounds great, but we will see when it happens. I don't expect any kind of relationship at this point, but I do hope he can change and be a good dad for Brianna.

November 1, 2004

BOTH of my parents and I decided to move into this townhouse together. It's crazy. I thought them driving in a car together was extreme, but this is a whole new level. It's a cute 3-bedroom place and really cheap, especially split 3 ways. It kind of works for everyone since they can probably watch the baby for me at different times, and my dad doesn't have a car right now, so he can use mine. I'm excited for Brianna and me to have our own space and a real living room and kitchen.

December 3, 2004

Every time things start getting normal, some new shit has to happen. Can't things just be boring for a while???

The place I was working at is about to close down. The bar side is staying open, but they don't need any of the back office people anymore, so my job is gone. Now I need to go apply for unemployment and start looking for a job. This is so stressful, and we just moved into this new place.

December 12, 2004

Well, I finally have some good news. I found a daycare for Bri, and it's practically free because my income at this new job is so low that we qualified for food stamps and a daycare voucher. I got this part-time job at a dive bar around the corner. It's pretty shitty, but hopefully the tips are good. It reminds me of Hard Times, and I'm pretty sure half the people there are tweaked out of their minds or doing lines in the bathroom. Hell, we know I can see all the signs. It actually makes me a little sick working there and seeing it from the outside now. I don't really have many choices, though. I need to make some money, and I hate to send Brianna to daycare, but what are my options?

December 19, 2004

My mom and I took these pictures at this photographer's house today. I can't wait to see them when we get back. We are going to use them to promote her shot business. She has all these young girls that she pays to go to bars and pass out shots. For Halloween, we all dressed up like nurses and gave out shots in a syringe. A little ironic, LOL, but it was cool. We each made a couple hundred bucks that night. Anyway, she wanted us to do these sexy pictures in bathing suits and lingerie to help promote it. The guy was kind of weird, and I felt really self-conscious being half-naked in front of this stranger, but at least my mom was with me. In one shot, he had me get my hair and shirt wet, and you could practically see through it! I just tried using my arms to cover up. At least I'm feeling skinny again. I guess that's one thing about having a kid while you're young. You literally don't have to worry about the weight coming off. Alright, well, I'm going to bed. Talk to you soon.

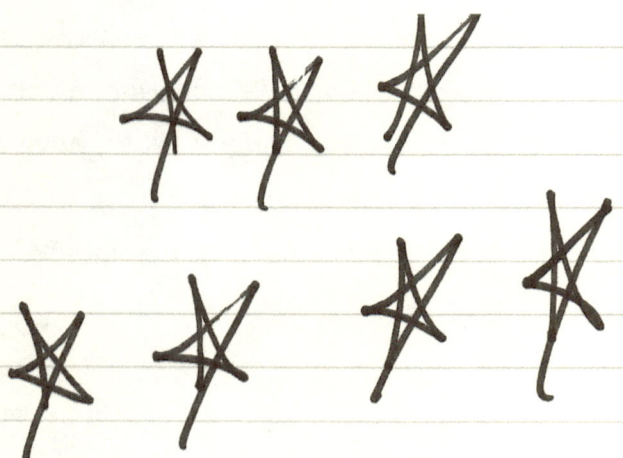

PART 3: GROWTH

FINDING MY VOICE

December 26, 2004

I think I'm going to start writing notes and letters to Brianna. I'll put them in here for now, and one day I'll put them all together in a journal for her and give it to her when she is older.

~~~~~~~~~~~

Letter to My Daughter

Brianna,

First, I'd like to tell you about me and your dad. We met in October of 2003. We started dating only a few days after we met, and I moved in with him shortly after that. In January, we moved in with his uncle, and on Valentine's Day, we found out I was pregnant with you! You should have seen the look on his face when I told him. He was so thrilled. He didn't know what to do with himself. We would stay up at night talking about what you would be like and how we would raise you. I remember one time he put his hand on my stomach, and you kicked. He said he thought you might be a soccer player. We were very much in love, but things started getting hard. He was working all the time, we didn't have our own place to live, and I couldn't get a job because we didn't have a car and I was pregnant. I decided it would be best if I moved in with Grandma back in Delaware. I wanted to make the right decision so that you could have the best life possible. I was by no means leaving your father. Once I moved to Delaware, though, we started growing apart. He called less and didn't understand why I had moved. I got a job and a place to live and was saving money so I could be prepared to give you the things you need and deserve. His mom and sister were there for us through the pregnancy, and they even came to see you after you were born. A month after you were born, I went to visit them in Virginia, and your dad saw you for the first time. He cried, which I've never seen before. He wanted us to begin a relationship again, but I told him it wouldn't be a wise choice and that I would love for him to be in your life. Since that day, we haven't talked. I know he loves you, but I think he is confused. I hope by the time you are reading this, the two of you have a close relationship. No matter what happens with him, I will never stand in the way of you getting to know each other. I never want you to feel bad for wanting to see him or think you can't speak openly about him. He is your family, and nobody can take that from you. Don't be afraid to ask questions. I promise to answer them truthfully.

December 30, 2004

Christmas was so nice. I got Bri a bunch of gifts, even though she is never going to remember this time, LOL. She is just the happiest little baby. Sometimes I think I don't even deserve her. I need to do better for her. I gotta snap out of this sad stuff. It's hard, though. I'm trying to make sure my parents aren't arguing or getting on each other's nerves. My dad has his life problems, and my mom is always dealing with something. I feel like I have to balance everything and take care of everyone else, so then I never really get to take care of myself. I don't even know what taking care of myself means. I really just want to spend all of my time with the baby and taking care of her. She is the only thing that matters. I guess it's not all bad, but everyday just feels like a struggle. Maybe if I write it out, I can tackle things one at a time.

Pros	Cons
I have a job	Car insurance getting canceled
I have a place to live	Dating sucks
Car is working	Living with my parents
Perfect baby	Nobody to help with the baby
	Bills and debt (student loans, credit cards, bank/bad checks)

January 2, 2005

I'm so confused. I can't believe this fucking happened. Of course, I'm concerned for my dad, but I'm also really pissed at him because I have NO CAR now. He is in the hospital and fine, of course, but he could have DIED. And if someone else had been in the car with him, they would certainly be dead. He quite literally wrapped my car around a tree. You know what's even crazier??? I let the insurance lapse two days ago because it was too much fucking money, so now...now, nothing. That's just it. No insurance, no help, no car, no nothing. I can't get to my shitty job without a car, and it doesn't make sense to take the bus or a taxi because of the amount of time it would take. And how the hell am I getting Brianna to daycare? I'm devastated. Literally just broken.

February 14, 2005

I don't know what happened. I really don't know what got into me. My mom and I were supposed to go work an event at the bar last night. It was for Valentine's Day and we were going to sell shots and roses. The thing is, I was still pissed at her for what happened earlier in the day. She had all this cash from different events lying on the table and had accused me of stealing it. ME?? SERIOUSLY, ME? Why would she even say that? I have NEVER stolen from her, and I've been clean for almost a year. Shit, she doesn't even know the dumb shit I stole before, but why would I steal from my mother? That's just stupid. I was so pissed. It started making me think I would never recover from all of this, that it's worthless and pointless because no matter what I do, I'll always be seen as an addict. Then I started thinking of Brianna and how she would be better off without me. I mean, I love her, and I try to be a great mom, but am I really gonna be good enough? She deserves so much better, and I thought if I weren't here anymore, then she would get what she needs somehow. I didn't really think it through well, but I knew somebody would be home in a couple of hours. I figured they would find me passed out/dead and could get Brianna. I put her upstairs in her crib so she would be safe and just started chugging vodka and whatever pain pills I could find in my mom's room. I really don't know what happened after that. Maybe I passed out from the alcohol, or my body just shut down? Next thing I know, they are pulling me out on a stretcher again, and then I'm getting my stomach pumped with that damn charcoal. They told me it was too late for me to drink it, and they would have to put the tube down my throat. My whole family came to visit, and my dad was sitting there crying. He felt so guilty for everything, I guess. It's not his fault, but all of these things definitely don't help. My head is spinning. I guess I really didn't WANT to die, but this is all too hard. I don't even know what happens from here. The doctors want me to stay. They are asking me if I want to go to the damn psych ward in the other wing of the hospital. I'm not sure what happens with Bri if I do that, but I feel like I have to go. I don't even know if they will let me leave if I want to.

February 16, 2005
Letter to My Daughter

COUNSELING

   I miss you more than anything right now. I am writing to you from an inpatient facility at Wilmington Hospital. I know it sounds crazy, and believe me, I don't feel like I belong here at all. At the same time, I know this will help me better myself so I can be the best mother possible for you. Let me explain a little. Since probably about age 14, I have suffered from clinical depression. I was never properly treated. I would self-medicate with drugs, but of course, that is only a temporary band-aid at best. Throughout the years, I have seen counselors on and off but never really took the steps to stabilize myself. Over the last 6 years, I have tried to commit suicide quite a few times. Whether it was with pills, drugs, antifreeze, or other methods. On February 12, 2005, I lost all hope. We had no car, which caused me not to be able to get you to daycare. I had to quit my job, and we have no money. We needed to move soon, and overall I was just overwhelmed. I tried to push through for you, but

I felt so alone. You were my only hope, the only thing I had worth living for. At the time, I thought you would be better off without me. Luckily, my tactics didn't work, and grandma found me and called the paramedics. Somehow, in some way, my body survived with no damage. I am now doing this therapy so I can be the best for you. I want to hold and kiss you so badly, but they only allow visitors every other day. I am doing my best to get out of here as soon as possible. I pray you will never feel this way. You are NEVER alone. I will always fight to the end for you. You deserve the best, and I will always be by your side cheering you on, picking you up when you're down, and patting you on the back. I pray you never have to deal with this and that I heal enough that we break this cycle in our family. I care about you more than you can ever imagine.

Love eternally, Mom

March 1, 2005

I'm finally out of that damn place. It was okay for a few days, but I started feeling crazy. Well, actually, I started feeling normal, and like the other people were too crazy for me to be around. Some of those girls were having psychotic breaks and screaming or fighting. It was wild. I just tried to stay to myself, write a lot, reflect a lot, and really think of what I need to get over all of this. At the end of the day, I just wanted to come home. I wanted to see my baby and do what I had to do to make this all work. We set up a plan, and I'm supposed to keep going to counseling and taking this medicine. It is like a happy pill. Every time I take it, I feel like I have a better day, so I guess it's working. It's crazy to think I used to take drugs to feel happy, and now I just take legal drugs to feel happy. Will there ever be a day I don't have to take anything and can feel happy? To be continued...

April 5, 2005

Okay, okay, everything is starting to turn around again. I got a new job thanks to my aunt, and it's even better than the one I had before!!! There is a lot of training, but it's at a bank, and I have to be on the phone all day. It pays pretty well, though, and I get insurance and all kinds of benefits. I probably won't qualify for

BABY GIRL :)

the daycare and food stamps now, but that's good because I don't want that stuff anyway, and that daycare was nasty. I was actually a little nervous about leaving Bri there every day. I'm so glad I didn't go to high school around here. It's like another fresh start. Everyone at this place seems to know each other from high school or growing up together, but I'm like the new girl. The good thing is none of them suspect anything about my old life. I can just pretend none of that happened and start a new chapter.

Oh yeah, and I started dating this other guy. I guess we are dating. Maybe we are boyfriend and girlfriend now? I don't know. He has a daughter too. The mom of his daughter is still around, but he sees his kid often. I like that he is so involved in her life. It's not like Brianna needs a new dad or anything, but it would be nice for her to have someone who is a good role model.

May 1, 2005

I still haven't talked to my mom. Honestly, ever since she accused me of taking that money, I just have a bad taste in my mouth. I can't make sense of it. How dare she throw that shit in my face? Especially when she has all these girls in the house all the time. Did she ask any of them if they stole it? Did she accuse them? Probably not. Just me, your own daughter. It's ridiculous. Then when everything happened and I was in the hospital, I felt like she just wanted me to hurry up and get home so I could take care of my responsibilities and she could get back to her own life. It's not like she was actually worried about me or what happened. We still don't talk about it either. We just all pretend nothing happened and keep going along with our shitty little lives.

July 16, 2005

I had enough. My dad and I moved out of the townhouse. I'm pretty sure my dad turned off all the utilities since they were in his name. My mom is going to flip. She will probably start blowing up my phone. Dave has this house and a second-floor apartment, so my dad is going to move upstairs, and Brianna and I can stay with Dave. There is plenty of room for all of us, and I can put a crib for Brianna in his daughter's room. His little girl is only a couple of years older than Bri, and they already love playing with each other. We also have a nice big yard now, and it's only 15 minutes from my work. The only thing about Dave is he smokes cigarettes, and I kind of picked up the habit again. Not all the time, but when Brianna is sleeping, I'll go outside and smoke one. I know it's awful and disgusting, but I need something. I feel a little more freedom now, though, since we moved out. I've got my own space again, and Dave doesn't care if I move things around a little bit. Hell, I barely have anything anymore. It's all just baby stuff and some clothes.

21 YEARS OLD

August 3, 2005

I'm going back to school. I didn't actually think I would ever go back, but my work reimburses us to take classes, so I might as well get my degree. The university has a combined bachelor's and master's program so I can get both in less than three years. I figure if I take night classes twice a week and do some online stuff, then I can actually pull it off. I just submitted my application so that I can register for fall classes. I can't wait!

August 11, 2005
Letter to My Daughter

DRUGS

This next topic is VERY important to me. I hope you do not read this and just brush it off. Drugs, alcohol, and cigarettes: I have done them all. I am an addict. I have been struggling with drugs for many years and probably will be for many more. Luckily, you have been the reason why the struggle has eased. You gave me a reason to stop. I knew your life was more important than mine, but at the same time, you needed a mother who would be there for you, not running off and doing drugs all the time. I know it will be hard for you and awkward, but I beg you to come talk to me before you try anything. I PROMISE I will not be mad or judge you. It's normal to be curious and experiment, but I know the danger that comes along with it, and I don't want you to have to experience it like I did. You might be thinking, "Screw you, I'll try it for myself and find out." If that's what you need to do, then I can't stop you, but I'd like you to be as safe as possible. I need you to know you can always be open with me and trust that I will love you no matter what. I will always listen. Unfortunately, addiction runs in our family, which makes having a decent life while using drugs nearly impossible. I tried many times to prove this fact wrong, but in the end, I realized that if it weren't for you, I would have lost just about everything because of drugs.

DISCOVERING INDEPENDENCE

January 3, 2006

I got the promotion at my job! I'm moving up from the phones to quality assurance. Basically, I get to give feedback to everyone on the phones. It's a little awkward since everyone knows me and we are all friends. Now I have to tell them when they are doing something wrong or making a mistake. I'm excited, though! It's more money, and of course, more responsibility.

February 12, 2006

I'm loving this mom life. My dad and I are living together in this cute little townhouse right in Trolley. Oh, I don't think I told you; we had to move out of Dave's. That shit was toxic, and I found out he was cheating with his daughter's mom, or his baby mama. He was actually lying to both of us, and we ended up finding out, becoming friends, and calling him out on his nonsense. Anyway, that's a whole long story in itself, but we moved out and found our own spot.

We got this cute little two-bedroom right off the main

road in town, and I can walk with Bri to the grocery store, and we actually have a front yard to play in. Bri even has her own mini room right off the back of my room. Im going to plant a little flower garden when the weather gets nicer. Things are finally coming together. We aren't allowed to have dogs here, so we got a small little mouse as a pet. That sounds ridiculous since most people try to get mice out of their house, and here we are buying one to bring in. They say they are good with small children and don't smell bad like guinea pigs. I don't know why I do this to myself and make more work and have another thing to clean up after, but I wanted Brianna to have a cute animal. She is the happiest little baby. Last night I was dancing with her while I was cooking dinner. She was so cute bouncing around and bopping her head. It felt like a scene from a movie. <3

March 1, 2006

I wanna thank me! Yeah, that's right. I've come a long way in the last couple of years. Part of me is amazed at how quickly I can go into the deep, dark, scary parts of life and then pull myself out. It's almost like a game. I wonder if there is ever a place I could get to that I won't be able to get myself out of. I often wonder why I put myself in those situations, too. What is the point of being miserable and unhappy? Am I TRYING to hurt myself and be lazy, or is that just how life is? Maybe I'm overthinking it. I'm just glad I've gotten to the place where I am today and can leave those old parts in the past.

March 16, 2006

"Got a box of sharp objects. What a beautiful day!" —The Used

I met a guy today. He's not really my type at all. I don't even know if I have a type. We didn't even really start talking, or rather flirting, until the very end of our time together. My work took us all on a chartered field trip to Atlantic City. I don't even know who planned or organized it, but it was nice to get out together and walk the boardwalk, take shots, and gamble. My friend Scott was our group leader in a way, making sure everyone was happy and laughing the whole time. It was a much-needed break for me, not having to worry about my daughter and getting a day all to myself. I finally feel like myself again. My quirky side is back. I was skipping down the boardwalk making silly jokes, funny faces, and rocking my new haircut and blue eyeshadow. It's the first time in a long time that I don't care what other people think, and I'm confident about who I am. I think I'll always have that little part inside of me that cares what people think, but I really feel good, like everything is locked in and I'm living a normal life. I don't even think I noticed Jason for half the day, LOL. I wasn't really paying attention to him at all. The whole bus was full, but our small group was walking together all day, and he was just kind of quiet. I guess I thought he was kind of cute, but he didn't really engage in conversation, so I barely paid him any mind. On the bus ride home, he was sitting behind me. Then his phone rang, and it was a song from "The Used." "Sharp Objects" is one of my favorite angry songs from my drug days driving alone on dark, back roads, screaming at the world all the harsh things that have happened to me. I whipped my head around at top speed in total surprise, which started a conversation. We pulled back up to the parking lot and exchanged numbers. I guess the rest will be history. He has this red convertible two-seater. It looks really nice and expensive. You can tell he drives it with confidence, and maybe it makes him a little cocky. He owns a townhouse not too far away. I'm not saying we are going to be in a whole relationship, but I do like that he is stable and makes his own money. He works at a bank too, so I know he has to make decent money like me. He doesn't seem to mind that I have a kid either, and that's a plus because I'm definitely not gonna date a guy who can't see himself being a dad.

22 YEARS OLD

June 13, 2006

Floyd is basically out of the picture for good. I feel bad for Brianna. Now she doesn't get to have a real dad. I haven't heard a peep from him in so long, but I still wonder about him sometimes and if he will ever change. I don't get it. How do you just literally abandon your girlfriend and child? I'm sure he is still wrapped up in the drug life, but your family is trying to keep in touch, and you just fell off the face of the earth.

Things have been going so well with Jason. He really makes me feel safe and secure. He is definitely not the type that's going to hit me or leave me stranded on the side of the road like those other assholes. I just love that we do little family stuff together. He met Brianna the other day and was so cute with her. We take trips to the park and the mall, just normal shit. I'm actually happy for once, and I want it to continue.

September 1, 2006

It feels like it's all happening so fast, but really, it's just good timing. The lease at the house with my dad was up, so Bri and I decided to move in with Jason. Today was the big moving day! I'm so excited for all of the possibilities. I guess he bought this place with his ex-fiancée, but honestly, you would never know it. I haven't seen a trace of her here—not even a picture.

He keeps the house so nice and clean, and I love that. I used to think I was clean, but this guy is next level. Now I need to watch myself and make sure I'm not leaving crumbs or a mess. I don't want to be annoying, especially since I'm coming into his space. I have to make sure Brianna doesn't make a mess. I mean, she's only 2 years old, so she doesn't know any better. I always make sure we pick up after ourselves. Sometimes after I clean up, he still comes behind me and vacuums or sweeps. I guess he just wants to help. All the toys must stress him out too, because sometimes when Bri is playing, he follows the trail of toys behind her and puts them away in the bin. It's kind of cute, but then she just goes and grabs more to sprawl across the floor. It cracks me up!

I've never met a guy who had his shit together like this. I guess we are really building a future together. We both have solid jobs and cars, and now we live together. It's gonna be awesome.

December 28, 2006

Things have been quiet. Not much to share right now,
but we did have our first Christmas together, and it was too
cute. We even went shopping at IKEA and got Bri some new
bedroom furniture so she could have a little toddler bed. Now
we have a tree ornament with all three of our names on it.
It's all just normal stuff. I love that I don't have to worry
so much anymore. Things just feel regular, like a normal life.
I'm laughing because I don't even know what a normal life
is. The closest thing I can compare it to is TV, I guess. We go
to work, hang out with friends, make dinner, and that's it.
Nothing fancy, nothing dramatic. Just living. It's nice that he
takes care of all the finance stuff, too. My stuff was out of
control before when I didn't have a job and I got all those
collections and past due accounts. Now I just let him figure
it out, and he tells me the best thing to do with my 401k,
savings, and all that. I've never had any of this stuff before,
so I'm glad he knows what the heck he is doing.

March 8, 2007

I've been thinking a lot lately about all of my past
relationships. They were so abusive. I did not see it at the
time, but I was just reliving everything I saw with my mom.
I thought that stuff was normal. Now that I'm with Jason,
I know that is not how people should be treated. Stabbing

pencils, burning someone, or pulling their hair? It's insane. He barely even gets mad at me for anything. He does crack these little jokes sometimes that I don't like, but I'm probably just being sensitive. He will say he "pulled a Crystal" any time he makes a mistake or does something dumb. It's kind of his way of making fun of me, but I think he must believe it's cute. I can see him huffing and puffing when the house is messy, too. I know I'm not that messy, but we have a toddler living here, and you can only keep it so clean before losing your mind. Anyway, I'm not complaining. I feel really grateful to have him in our lives.

Letter to My Daughter

MEN

   I think you should know the women in our family have a history of being abused by men. This includes physically, mentally, and emotionally. Your great-grandmother, grandmother, and I have all been through it. I hope you will never feel this pain. You should know you are worth more than that. No man deserves to ever lay a hand on you or put you down, even if he says he loves you. There is no exception to this rule. Love is not supposed to hurt. At 22 years old, I am just now learning this. I'm currently trying to build my confidence so that nobody can knock me down. I hope you can learn from my mistakes and not let history repeat itself.

You are beautiful and amazing. When you know this in your heart and soul and believe it about yourself, nobody can make you feel otherwise.

23 YEARS OLD

June 17, 2007

Sorry I haven't been writing as much. Things have been good! I feel bad I only write in here when it's super good or super bad, but I guess that's a good thing that it's been quiet for a bit. Jason and I are really happy. Bri is in an amazing daycare, and work is great. They do want to test her for speech issues because she has been delayed with her talking, and potty training has been a bit of a mess!

Oh, and I did have this little issue a while ago where some girls at work found my anonymous online journal and figured out it was me. I didn't say anything that bad, but it did talk a lot about my past and had some gossip in it, so I just started deleting ALL the entries. I was bawling my eyes out to my boss because they had to pull me in and tell me what happened. I wasn't getting fired, but I could have. That would have been horrible, so I just started erasing EVERYTHING!! I'm glad I still have you, though, because I'm not ready to let all of those memories just disappear like that. This is my life! Anyway, other than that, nothing to report. TTYL!

August 1, 2007

So Jason and I have been talking about long-term stuff, and he wants to sell his townhouse because the market is really good; plus, we want a place of our own. Sooooo, we decided to start designing and building our own house. I hate to move again, but this is PERMANENT. Like, no more moving after this. We picked a perfect corner lot, and now we just have to design everything. He is going to use the money he makes from the townhouse as our down payment, and that will bring the mortgage payment down enough for us to split everything else.

I know Brianna doesn't realize it yet, but she is really going to have a great life, one I could have only dreamed about when I was her age.

September 2, 2007

We sold the townhouse faster than expected, and the new house isn't built yet. Jason's parents let us move in with them, but it's been intense. They are even cleaner than he is, and we have to take our shoes off and put on fresh socks when we walk in the door. You can't even go to the mailbox, come back inside, and sit on the couch. You have to shower or sit on the floor. I'm pretty sure his mom vacuums every single day. The house never looks dirty, so I'm not sure what she is even cleaning.

September 10, 2007

My dad's dad—my grandfather—passed away the other day. I'm not sure how to feel. This is really the first person I've ever known to pass away, and I barely knew him. Jason's mom won't leave me the hell alone and keeps coming to our room to try and clean or vacuum. I took the day off work to figure out what the hell I was feeling, but she wouldn't leave me alone. I should have just gone to work or at least left this house! I'm still so confused because I'm not sad, but I do feel a loss. Then I feel guilty for not feeling sad while at the same time feeling like I have no right to actually be sad since I barely knew him. Let's just say I'm definitely confused.

October 13, 2007

You'll never guess what happened! I think I'm still in shock. Jason asked me to MARRY HIM TODAY! I could hardly believe it myself. We just moved into the new house, OUR HOME!!! It was our first day here, and he called me upstairs to our bathroom. Honestly, my heart jumped a little because he had that disappointed voice. He told me to come look at the countertop in the bathroom. I thought something was wrong with the way he called my name. I rushed upstairs in a panic and went straight to the bathroom counter, fearful I had scratched it while putting the new stuff away.

Then I saw it—a sparkly ring sitting in a black box!! I must have looked so surprised. He smirked and said, "Well?" Of course, I said yes, and the ring is just beautiful. I can't stop staring at it. I really wasn't even expecting it. We never really talked about marriage, but our life has been tracking that way since we met—we were dating, then moved in together, built this house, and basically have a kid together, so marriage is the obvious next step. I guess I'm planning a wedding now!

November 11, 2007

We've met a bunch of the neighbors now. It's so nice to have friends close by. It's like a dream—picture-perfect life, coming right up! There is one couple that lives right down the street and two more that we have been hanging out with who live around the corner. Every weekend is full of laughs, games, annnnd drinking, LOL. The kids all play in the basement together, and it's like having our own little crew.

December 22, 2007

I'm starting to have questions. Holidays are weird. Why don't we see Jason's family? They didn't spend Thanksgiving with us, and we only saw them briefly for Christmas. Maybe they aren't as close as I thought or are just busy. I was hoping for more, but I can't say much when my family doesn't really see each other anymore either.

March 1, 2008

We decided to make the wedding sooner, but nobody besides our 2 witnesses knows we are getting married on March 16th. We were planning our wedding for next year, but we are going to say our vows this month so Jason can adopt Brianna. Her biological dad has been threatening to come back into our lives, and I'm afraid he will steal or take her one day. This protects everyone. I think Jason is stressed. It's probably all of this wedding stuff and planning for the big day. He told me today he didn't like how I drink water and that it's disgusting, loud, and annoying.

May 4, 2008

Life is great. We don't actually have a white picket fence, but it sure feels like it. This is seriously the life I always dreamed of—a single-family home with a yard, friends in the neighborhood, backyard BBQs, bike rides, and a swimming pool down the road. I love all the family things we do together.

July 17, 2008

My self-doubt is starting to kick in. Jason always seems annoyed or bothered by me or Brianna. After I wipe down the counters, he interrogates me like I didn't do it or I'm lying. I literally don't see what he sees. It's like there are invisible crumbs he wants me to clean off. I've been trying to be a really good wife and make sure I have dinner cooked and ready every night and keep everything tidy. It's tough, though, with work and making sure I get time to play with Brianna. There are a lot of things pulling at me, and I just want him to be happy.

Brianna is starting to catch on too and is trying to keep her stuff clean. The other night when the garage door started to go up, she and I both jumped and started cleaning her toys off the floor. It wasn't that messy, and we were still playing, but I didn't want him to walk in the door and be angry or bothered by us. It was easier just to clean it up for now. I just have to do a better job. He does so much to make sure we are taken care of and pays most of the bills. I feel like it's my duty to at least keep the house clean. I'm working on it.

September 19, 2008
Letter to My Daughter

CONFIDENCE

Brianna, another thing to remember is you should always be who you are. Don't change yourself for anyone. You are the one who has to live with yourself every day. You should be satisfied with what you become. The fact is, no matter how hard you try, you can never become perfect for anyone. Even if you changed everything they asked, neither one of you would be happy in the end. You are perfect for someone just the way you are! Someone who truly loves you will love the best things about you and love you even more for the things that aren't so perfect. So just be you! <3

October 5, 2008

We got married yesterday (again—haha). It was so beautiful. Everything turned out perfectly. 120 of our closest friends and family were there, the weather was great, and no major catastrophes occurred. Before the wedding, I could see our family waiting outside for me to walk down. I was surprised at how calm I felt throughout the whole day. I thought people normally have wedding day jitters, but I had none. I guess that's a good thing! I don't know any happily married couples anyway, so maybe that's why, LOL. This is the happiest I've ever been. Sure, Jason has his quirks, but he means well. Plus, he takes care of all our finances to make sure the bills get paid. It's nice to have a partner to do some of the "adult" stuff that I don't know how to do. My job is decent, but I'm glad he organizes the other life stuff so I don't have to worry about it.

PURPOSE AND PASSION

November 13, 2008

Well, guess who started their own business? Me! Yep, I figure I already learned how to do all of the planning for our wedding, so I might as well make a business out of it and do it for other people too. It's called All About Events. I'm focused mostly on weddings right now, but I'll do any type of event. I'm excited to have something that's my own and can be proud of. Honestly, all the wedding planning stuff came naturally, so this feels like an easy step. Okay, well, I've gotta finish building the website and designing my business cards. Talk later!

January 7, 2009

Here we go again. Jason is just so annoyed. We barely saw his family during the holidays, and we didn't really see any of my family, either. Nothing I do seems to make him happy, and I feel like I'm always walking on eggshells. I can't tell if it's him or me, but I just try to stay out of his way. We were going to start trying to have a baby, but it's not like we have much intimacy right now. He just seems so distant. Constantly angry and so disappointed or annoyed with me.

January 16, 2009

We all went ice skating today. It was Bri's first time, and she loved it. She wobbled all over the place but cracked up the whole time. Jason didn't really want to skate, but he came with us, so that was nice. We all went out to eat afterward and got some hot chocolate. I think we are going to drive around and see if there are any more Christmas lights up in the neighborhood.

January 23, 2009

Ahhhhh! It's so funny how things work out. In one of my classes at the university, this girl was talking about the local roller derby team she started or has been running for a while. My ears perked up immediately! I love roller skating. I haven't even really done it since I was a teenager, but those were some of the best times going to the skating rink on the weekends. Roller derby is a bit more intense. She said I needed a helmet and elbow and knee pads. They practice late at night, so I could go after my Wednesday class when Bri is in bed and check it out. I'm gonna go next week and see if I like it. It would be nice to have something I enjoy doing and get some other friends outside of just our neighbors and people at work, ya know? Wish me luck!

February 13, 2009

Valentine's Day is tomorrow. I've never really had a "Valentine." Is that a thing? Do people actually do that? I don't think we are doing anything for each other tomorrow. Jason and I talked before, and we don't really celebrate it. I mean, it's a fake holiday anyway, and I don't need anything special. I know he loves me; he married me, right? LOL, I wouldn't be mad if he got me some flowers or chocolates, though. A girl still likes to be shown a little extra love. <3

March 1, 2009

Got a custom tattoo on my rib cage yesterday. I found this local guy who drew me the most perfect Phoenix. I thought it was appropriate given the meaning and symbolism—rising from the ashes, new beginnings, blah, blah, blah. I didn't tell Jason what it meant. He didn't seem like he cared much anyway. I actually think he was bothered that I was getting it. I thought he would want to come with me, but he just stayed home with Brianna. I feel like a new person. I've really had an evolution over the years. I'm still figuring out what the hell I'm doing, but today feels like I've drawn a line in the sand about what I want my life to be like.

March 22, 2009

    I am really in my groove. I got to plan my first really
big event. Our friends have a son who is going through
brain cancer. I wasn't really sure how to help them, but I
knew they needed money for all the surgeries and doctor
visits. I planned this huge beef and beer event. We ended up
having over 100 people there and raising close to $8,000!
I was so happy for them. Jason and I had to get up and
give a speech. I didn't really know what to say, and you
know I hate drawing attention to myself, but I just thanked
everyone for coming and Jason for helping (even though he
didn't even really help, LOL, unless you want to count him
watching Brianna while I planned everything). I guess that
counts. I'm really happy it went well, and now I have a
ton of confidence going into the wedding season, so I can
start promoting my business. I already had two consults for
some medium-sized weddings, and I think they are going to
book. My prices are pretty cheap right now since I have no
experience. I am a little scared to death that I'm going to
ruin someone's wedding, though.

March 23, 2009

    Ugghhhhh, I don't want to forget this stuff. I keep
thinking how he acts is okay and it's all my fault, but maybe
writing it down will help me remember how I feel right now.

He doesn't provide any emotional support and despises everything I do:

- Charity events
- My job
- That I go to school
- Roller derby
- The way I drink water—apparently if the bottle crinkles, I'm annoying
- The way I drive
- Any time I'm happy or dance and sing with Brianna (one of my favorite things to do!)
- The music I like
- When I ask too many questions

March 30, 2009

This might sound crazy, but I've been thinking about divorce lately. It feels really extreme, but things are just not the same as they were before. I can't ever be my quirky self around Jason. He looks at me like he is disgusted any time I try to do something funny or silly. If Bri and I are playing or making crazy faces and singing songs, he looks at me out of the side of his eye in utter disappointment. Then don't even get me started on the yelling and condescending comments. Before, I blamed it on his stress over the wedding or work, but it just never stops. I don't even know how divorce would really work. Maybe if I brought it up to him, he would start working on it. Jeez, we just celebrated one official year of marriage, and now it's like our life has been flip-flopped upside down. How did things go from so perfect to so icky that quickly?

April 5, 2009

I did it. I brought up the divorce thing today with Jason, and he freaked out. I had printed out the papers that tell you what to do and how you have to be technically separated for 6 months. He practically lunged towards me. It scared the shit out of me. I've never seen him get that mad. I tried to stay calm, but he just kept yelling and freaking out. He refuses to try any sort of counseling and thinks everything is fine. I told him I don't like the way he talks to me or deals with Bri, but he just acts like I'm crazy. Then he talks about all the stuff I do wrong and how I shouldn't even be talking to him about what he does because of my past. I don't know what to do now, and I'm scared. I don't feel safe with him at this point and started moving all of my stuff into the spare room. I got a blow-up bed from the basement, put my clothes in the other closet and moved my stuff out of our bathroom and into the hallway bathroom. At least now I feel like I have some space to myself and a way to get away from him.

April 16, 2009

It's wedding season time! I've been so busy. I'm planning for 3 weddings this May. It's going to be epic. It's cool to think I'm going to be one of the reasons someone has an easy and happy day. I still get nervous meeting clients and wonder if they question whether I know what the hell I'm talking about, LOL. I just fake it half the time and then go find the answers later. I guess just showing them my confidence and making them feel comfortable has gone a long way in locking in these jobs. It's a bit of pressure sometimes, but the outcome makes it all worth it. I wonder if I could do this full-time one day.

April 22, 2009

I told Jason I wanted to start going to AA or NA meetings. He thinks it's a bad idea. He looked at me like I had three heads when I told him about it. He doesn't know much about my past, but I did tell him I had a problem with drugs before Brianna was born. He never really asked questions, and I didn't give him many details. It's been tough these last few years managing my addictive personality. I don't think I would ever go back to it—drugs, but I know I need to figure out what caused me to even go to that dark place to begin with. There is still something inside of me that longs for something else to fill that void. It's like a deep, dark pit inside of me that can't be filled.

May 12, 2009

I've gotten to a breaking point. I'm honestly more scared for Bri than myself. I don't think Jason has the guts to actually do anything physical to me, but I see him escalating and I'm worried he will hurt her. What if he just snaps one day? And forget the physical part; all of the verbal and emotional abuse is enough! Nobody should jump or tighten their whole body when they hear their dad coming.

I'm going to talk to him about doing a trial separation to see how it is for everyone. I'll take Bri and stay in a hotel for a week. I'm not sure what I'm looking for or what it will be like, but I'm hoping we all get a little peace, and maybe it will scare him enough to know that I can leave and he will straighten up. I don't actually want to get a divorce. I don't even know how I could do it, but I can't live like this.

May 22, 2009

I was shocked he even agreed to this but now I know why. This damn trial week is not going how I planned. Why do I still need him? I keep having to call him for everything. The first night Brianna and I went to dinner, and then we locked ourselves out of our hotel room. Out of instinct, I called him first. I didn't even go to the front desk of the hotel yet. Oh, and it's the worst hotel, some little Budget Inn, a rinky-dink place. It's actually kind of scary and not comfortable at all. We are eating takeout and using a tiny refrigerator. It's dark and gloomy and I miss all of our stuff.

25 YEARS OLD

June 3, 2009

Now that we are back at the house, I've been going to roller derby practice, and it's really making me feel alive again. I decided not to go to the NA meetings. I remember when I used to go with Kevin in high school and a bunch of people smoked and hung out outside. I actually think it would give me access to stuff I wouldn't otherwise try to find. Roller derby has been a healthy new addiction. We only practice twice a week, and it doesn't really take away from my time with Brianna. One is late at night, and the other one is super early on the weekend. They call us "fresh meat" since we are newbies trying to make it onto the team. The other night, they threw literal bags of trash onto the rink, and we had to jump over them. It was terrifying, but I did it! I was so proud of myself for conquering my fear and just going for it.

July 11, 2009

We have been talking about trying for another baby. I wonder if it would make things better for us. I know that's a dumb reason to have a baby and definitely not the only one, but I'm ready to be a mom again. Now that Floyd is out of the picture for good and we have our own house, stable jobs, and enough money, it feels like it all makes sense. I'm sure Jason would like a kid of his own, and he has been talking about it lately. I think it could make him a better father overall. I really just want us all to be happy.

August 2, 2009

Ugh! I don't know why he always does this. Every time I'm about to go to practice, he starts picking little fights with me. It's like he doesn't want me to be happy. He KNOWS I have derby practice every Wednesday, yet every week when I'm about to head out, he starts nagging me about something. It's literally 8 o'clock at night! What is there to be annoyed about? We hardly spend real time together watching shows. He wants to watch sports, and I'm trying to watch a comedy show. I don't get it. It's not like he misses me and wants me to stay home. I'm starting to think he just doesn't want me to have fun with anyone else. It makes me a little worried to leave Bri home alone with him when he gets like that. I mean, what would he do if he is trying to get her to bed and she gives him a hard time? I've seen what happens when that switch goes off, and I would never forgive myself if he did anything to her. Derby has been my escape, my place to just BE. Be silly, be confident, be curious, be alone.

I really don't want him to take that from me and now I'm so conflicted.

October 2, 2009

    We've still been trying to get pregnant, but no luck yet. We decided to make an appointment at the fertility clinic to make sure everything was okay. It's only been a couple of months, but I had all those problems when I was younger with bad exams and the one time they had to do a biopsy. It's crazy to think about now because I was like 16, and they were just cutting out pieces of my body without my parents knowing. How is that even legal??? Now I wonder if it could have damaged something and I didn't know it. Jason is almost 30 years old and has never had a baby or gotten anybody pregnant, so I guess it's good to check all of these things to be sure.

November 3, 2009

    He is still being a jerk, but I guess this is just how things are now. Maybe it's not as bad as I think. As I sit here and think about it, I don't know ANY other happy couples. We are probably the happiest I know, and that's not saying much. Literally every person we know seems annoyed with their partner, and they bicker constantly. The other couples always seem like someone else is cheating or they just hate each other. At least we keep it pretty quiet, and most of the rudeness is done behind closed doors. I don't want my friends to know about our issues, and then we make up and they still think he's a jerk, ya know?

Is this really what it's like to be married, though? Is this what everyone goes through? I'm trying to figure out if it's normal to argue with your spouse like this and feel like you're not good enough. Maybe it's just me. Maybe I'm being dramatic or too emotional. I don't even know if I'm IN LOVE. I love him, but I just don't feel those butterflies I always promised myself. Do people actually feel them once they have been together for a while? I really should just be happy that things aren't crazy. My life really isn't bad compared to all the shit I was going through before.

December 26, 2009

Christmas was so fun. Bri is so happy, and we were able to give her so many presents. Jason got another raise, and I was promoted to another department as a project manager. We honestly don't even worry about money at all, which is something I never thought would exist in my life.

We are thinking about getting me a new car, probably an SUV, because once we get pregnant, it will be a lot easier to have a bigger car where I can pile all the "stuff" in it since I'm sure I'll be taking the kids everywhere.

February 20, 2010

We took the skills assessment for roller derby, and I PASSED!!!! That means I'm out of the "fresh meat" stage and actually get to be placed on one of the teams. I've been obsessed with the movie *Whip It* ever since it came out, too. It's all about derby!! I wish I could skate like that. It's so freeing to race around the track without a care in the world.

The best part is I can't overthink or think about anything except for skating. All the thoughts in your mind are just quiet, and it's nothing but you and the track—and the girls chasing you down, LOL. I wish I could bottle up that feeling and pull it out whenever I want.

SILVER SPLATHER!!!

March 24, 2010

Ugh, I had a horrible night of sleep, and then I woke up to an email with bad news :(I had applied to this teaching program that I wanted to be a part of, and they rejected me. It felt so harsh. I guess I can apply next year, but I was really looking forward to it. It kind of broke my heart a little bit.

April 12, 2010

Guess who is pregnant?!?!!? We didn't even need the treatments, it just happened on its own right before we started the medication. I'm so excited! I think Jason is too. I really did not want to take those hormone shots, and I'm so glad I didn't have to do any of that. Based on their calculations, she should be here in November! I can't believe I'm going to be a mom of TWO.

PART 4: BECOMING

ACCEPTANCE

26 YEARS OLD

June 1, 2010

I was talking to my boss the other day. She has two girls. I was telling her how scared I am about my kids thinking I love one more than the other. I just can't imagine how you make sure each kid knows you love them the same. I mean, I guess it's different, but it's not like you love one kid more than the other. She told me how there will always be one child that is more like you or maybe easier to understand or get along with, but as long as you love them each for who they are, then you can never go wrong. It definitely made me feel better. I feel like that's something I can do, and I can't wait for Bri to have a sibling.

Oh, and I had to stop roller derby. I probably could have skated a little longer, but I was nervous that it was going to be too dangerous. I definitely can't get hit or knocked to the ground. I'm sad, but I know it's the right choice. Plus, now I can just focus on growing this little baby.

July 19, 2010

Jason and Bri got to feel the baby kick today! Their faces were priceless.

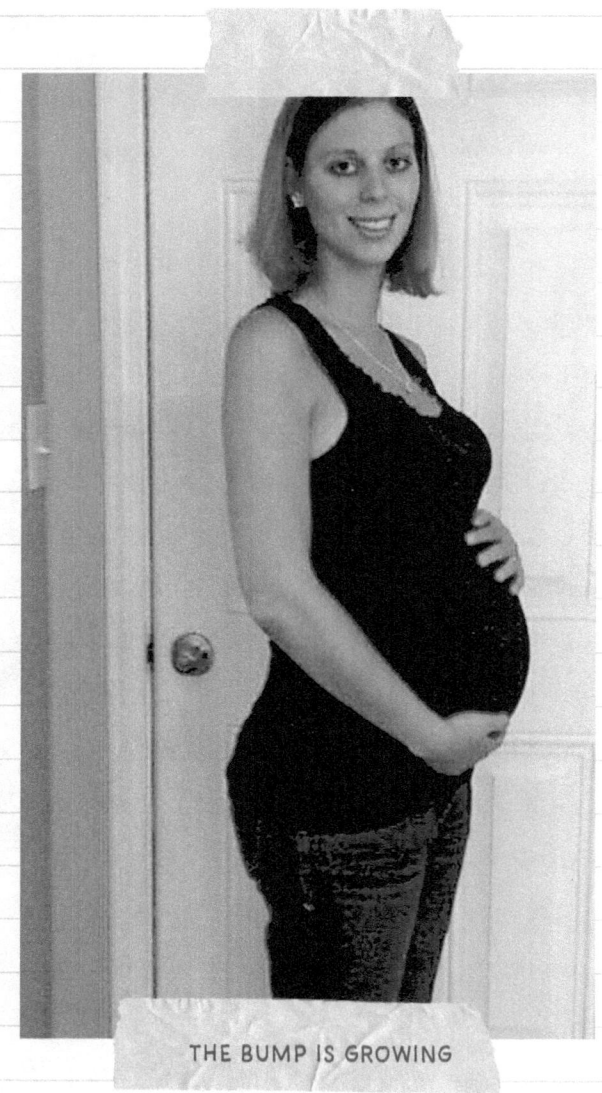

THE BUMP IS GROWING

July 31, 2010

I'm getting so huge! I'm over this pregnancy thing. It's definitely not as easy as it was when I was 19! Let's not even talk about the heat. I'm over it.

August 15, 2010

Today is the big day! I've been planning the first-ever Suicide Prevention Walk in Delaware, and I've got 1,000 people registered to walk. We already raised $6,000, and my work has a program where they match any funds you raise for charity, so that means $12k to help teach other people about ways to prevent suicide. It's definitely going to be a long day, but I'm really proud of this event. My stomach is huge, and I look like a whale, LOL. We have a DJ, snacks, and a few guest speakers. It's going to be epic!

September 2, 2010

I've been staying super busy, and it's nice to feel like a real mom. Is that weird? I feel like it's taken me a few years to get the hang of all this, and now that I'm going to be a mom of two, I want to do all the mom stuff! Bri started Girl Scouts and swim lessons. I've been cooking a lot more and doing house projects. It's just nice to feel like a real family.

November 3, 2010

I've been having lots and lots of dreams about the baby. I keep thinking she is going to come out a boy—even though all the ultrasounds say girl.

November 9, 2010

Baby girl #2 is here!!! Well, we thought we were going to deliver at the birthing center, but she had other plans! On Monday night I woke up several times, as usual, to go to the bathroom throughout the night. This time I felt a little crampy but figured if labor was imminent, I might as well get some rest, so back to bed I went. At 4:30 AM, I was awoken by slightly stronger contractions that were coming about 7 to 8 minutes apart, but I could still easily walk and talk. I let Jason continue to sleep, knowing his alarm would wake him up by 5:30, and if contractions were closer or lasting longer, then we could call the birth center. I asked him to work from home just in case but thought it could be a few hours. The contractions continued somewhat sporadically and longer, but there was more time between the contractions, so I decided to hold off on calling the midwives. By 9:15 AM, I gave them a call just to let them know what was going on and that I might be coming in later. They advised me to continue resting and call when I had more news. By 10 AM, contractions had altogether stopped, and I figured they must have been Braxton Hicks, so I might as well take a nap. Suddenly, at 12 PM, I started having quick contractions that only lasted 15–20 seconds apiece, but they were occurring every 3 minutes. I still wasn't sure this was actually "it" and expected them to stop. However, at 1 PM, I had a very painful contraction that lasted over a minute. The next one came 3 minutes later. I yelled to Jason to call the birth center now and that we had to get in the car right away! As I got in the car (without shoes or a coat), I felt an odd urge to go to the bathroom and ran back into the house just in time to have my water break. It literally splashed all over the bathroom floor. All I could think was, "Jason is going to be so pissed at this mess!" before grabbing a towel and running into the car.

Within minutes of the car ride, I told him we were not going to make it all the way to Wilmington and he needed to call the birth center. He was speeding through town, and I was beeping the car horn profusely to move cars out of our way. Clearly, they didn't know I was in labor!!!

The birth center told us to drive to the nearest hospital, but I knew we weren't going to make it.

Then I had the urge to begin pushing. Jason told me not to push like I had a choice, LOL. Now it was time to pull over and call 911.

The 911 operator told him I needed to lie somewhere flat. As I looked at the pebble-covered ground, I realized I had to find a way to the back of our NEW SUV. Keep in mind, at this point I am half naked, literally pants off, and all modesty has been thrown out the window. Jason puts the back seat down flat, and I rush to the trunk and scream for him to close it so the passing cars don't see all of the "excitement." Jason yelled for me to push, and within 2–3 pushes Miss Ashley arrived in the world. Immediately after she came out, 3 ambulances pulled up just in time to cut the cord and get us to the hospital. Needless to say, our car did not fare so well, though my wonderful OCD husband is dealing with it well.

For two people who plan every detail of their lives, this definitely was not the way we planned it, but I don't think we would ask for it to happen any other way. I think it would be safe to say that Ashley will decide how to do things on her time and nobody else's. That is for sure!

November 11, 2010

I know it's only been a day, but this labor feels so much different. Before I was a young, single mom without any stability, and now I have a family. I actually get three months off work to stay home and bond with her. I'm really excited to just put all of my energy into nourishing myself and the baby.

November 14, 2010

We've had to tell everyone the birth story repeatedly. I find it super odd that people always seem to compliment

Jason first on what a good job he did delivering the baby and how scary it must have been, blah, blah, blah. I keep thinking in my head, why aren't they giving me kudos for handling the most terrifying situation and actually giving BIRTH to the baby on the side of the road??? All he did was catch her. I don't say this to any of them, of course, but it just doesn't seem right.

November 26, 2010

Ahhhh, I got to go back to skating again tonight. I know some people think it's too soon, but I feel good, and I need this. Funny how they always tell moms to take time for themselves and "fill their cup," and then when you do it, everyone is judging you or telling you to "be careful," "take your time," "don't move too quickly," "aren't you going to miss the baby"... they seriously don't stop. Anyway, it was rough, and I was definitely a bit slower than usual, but it felt so good to be there.

December 2, 2010

Why didn't someone tell me about baby-wearing 6 years ago?? I just vacuumed and unloaded the dishwasher while carrying my baby, yet both hands were free! Hallelujah!

December 11, 2010

We have a packed day! First, the chiropractor. Did you know they can do pediatric chiropractic care too? Then I'm heading over to mentor a pregnant teen at one of our local schools. Afterward, I'm going to the moms' group. All of us moms had our babies around the same month, so we meet every month and talk about everything going on. Oh, then we have a baby dance class. I don't even know what that will be like, but I'm pretty sure we can wear our babies while we are dancing. I'll report back!

December 13, 2010

It's finally time! I'm submitting my application for this teaching program again. Ever since I started mentoring at the schools and volunteering on the weekends, I've felt this tug to change careers for real. I just KNOW this is my year. Now that Brianna is in school and I see some of the struggles she is going through, I want to make sure I know how to support her. It's just been really satisfying working with kids and getting to see them grow and progress because of the support and guidance I'm providing. I know it would be a huge pay cut if I switched careers, but Jason seemed fine with it. Actually, I think he probably doesn't even think I'll get in.

Well, I'm submitting all of my info tonight, and if—okay,

WHEN—I get in, I'll have to go to summer institute for 7 weeks to learn allllll of the things. Then when I get home, I'll officially be a teacher.

Wish me luck!!

December 19, 2010

Looking back at my life right after Bri was born, I think I was going through postpartum depression. I had no idea what that was before, but now it all makes sense. I mean, on top of the withdrawals I was probably having, leaving my whole life, and then taking care of a baby, I think I was just sad and lost. I have NONE of those feelings now. I am just loving every second of this time off work and no stress. Jason has been super chill, too. He definitely can't stand all of the bottles and rags everywhere, but he has been giving me a break and even cooking dinners. He gets a little stressed with Bri, but I've been able to step in and stop him from screaming or giving her a hard time. I think having the baby has really helped us, or at least helped him, calm down a little bit.

January 4, 2011

I was not expecting this. We just spent Christmas Eve baking cookies with my grandparents and great-grandmother. I'm so glad she got to meet Ashley and see Brianna again.

I just found out she passed away. Why the hell do we say passed away? That doesn't even convey the full meaning of what happened. She is gone. Dead. Not coming back. Nobody gets to see her anymore, learn her stories, taste her cooking, or watch her smile. She passed? That sounds like she took a test or just went away for a little bit. I'm not quite sure how to deal with all of this. Are people just going to keep dying? Do you ever get used to it? Is there a good way to deal with grief, or are we all just out here struggling?

January 13, 2011

I guess the baby moon phase is over. Jason is back at his usual bullshit. Every time he starts back up again, I think about how I should have left him sooner. Then I think it's not that bad. He isn't hitting me. He doesn't break things. Well, it does feel like my soul is breaking. Little by little, he takes my happy spirit and rips it to shreds, piece by piece. He keeps using my past against me too. It's like he knows I can't depend on my parents for things and I was a drug addict, so in his mind, that makes him better than me. I started writing a separate journal of notes of all the things he does so I don't forget or just brush them off. It's like as soon as a couple of days pass, it doesn't seem that bad. It's like I have amnesia. Then I think I must have done something to piss him off, or maybe I just imagined it worse than it was. Now, I won't forget.

January 22, 2011

I skipped girls' night today. I was supposed to go to Amy's to watch our show, but honestly, I was too scared to leave the kids home alone with Jason. I knew (well, I don't think) he would hurt the baby, but Brianna wasn't in bed yet and he was clearly on edge, so I just made an excuse and told the girls I wasn't feeling well. It's easier to nurse the baby at home anyway, and then I could snuggle with Bri and make sure she got to bed without getting yelled at.

January 30, 2011

I think he is insane at this point. He thinks our house is DIRTY when it's literally spotless. I can't keep up. My anxiety is on edge all the time. I'm constantly afraid I did something wrong, left something out, or didn't clean well enough. It's just absurd. All he cares about is cleaning and what the house looks like, but he doesn't even invite anyone over! It's not like anybody sees the damn house.

February 2, 2011

I NEED roller derby, but I swear he tries to pick these fights with me every single time before I leave the house. It will be over the dumbest thing, and then we are both arguing and screaming at each other. It reminds me of the stuff I used to see when I was a kid, and I hate it. Half the time, I'm scared to leave him alone with the kids because he is so wound up, so I end up staying home. I don't know what it is, but it's like he could snap at any moment. He has this look in his eyes when he gets angry, almost like he blacks out or is not here in this world. I never know what's going to happen next. He says the most vile things too. I started keeping my phone in my back pocket and recording voice memos. I just want to make sure I'm not making this stuff up because I don't think anyone would believe me if I told them the stuff he yells at us every day—constantly putting us down and saying how disgusting we are or worthless pieces of scum. He yelled at Brianna the other day and told her to just "sit in her pissy pants" because she was the problem. How is a six-year-old a problem? She is a CHILD!! I've definitely noticed how he treats the kids differently now too. Everyone said that would happen, but I didn't believe them. He has taken care of Bri since she was little and literally adopted her, but now I wonder if he shouldn't have done that—or if I shouldn't have let him adopt her. It seems like he resents her or is angry at her just for the way she is. She isn't a bad kid or mean. She makes regular kid mistakes like everyone else, but God forbid she spills some milk or makes a mess. He flips his lid! He needs everything perfect, in its place, or there is hell to pay. It just doesn't seem normal.

February 21, 2011

REMEMBER THE THINGS HE HAS SAID REFERRING TO BRI

- "She is fucking awful" "She is horrible" "She never gets it right"
- "She is being a fucking asshole that is going to bed"
- "It's probably your asshole"
- Mocking her "Yeah, I took the fucking gate. She is such a baby. Sit down and shut your mouth. Waa waa waaa."
- "Little fucking brat"
- "THERE IS A PROBLEM, AND HER NAME IS BRIANNA"
- "You can sleep in your own little piss puddle"
- "Tough shit. There could be eight rolls of toilet paper, and your ass would still look shitty"

WHAT ELSE HE HAS DONE

- Constant drinking, sleeping in, and reckless driving
- Controlling behaviors about money, my job, the TV, all furniture, the computer, iPad, iPhone
- Constant threats of suicide and attempts or saying he "won't be here anymore"

March 17, 2011

With all this craziness going on, at least I have something to look forward to! I got a call back from that teaching program, and now I have to do an in-person interview. I'm not even sure how to prepare, and I'm so nervous but also excited. This could be the first step into my new life, a happier life where I'm actually fulfilled and making a difference. All this time mentoring, I've felt like I'm actually helping, like my past is a way to help others not make the same mistake.

Who is going to be a teacher? This girl!! I didn't make it to this round last year, but it has to happen this year. It just has to. I've never wanted something so bad in my life.

March 25, 2011

If only I could bottle and sell the feeling after a good night of derby. I'd be rich, I tell ya!

The aftermath of a good scrimmage means that I can't quite bend my left leg. And yet, I still want to put on my skates today.

April 17, 2011

I called my friend Erin earlier today. She is going through a similar situation with her husband and getting a divorce. I wish I had opened up about all of this to her sooner. The good thing is when I told her, she didn't seem shocked. She actually seemed like she understood what I was going through. I was telling her how conflicted I was and that I didn't know how to leave. She reassured me to just take one step at a time and everything will fall into place. She wasn't necessarily telling me to leave him, but she told me she would support me in whatever decision I made and that I just needed to make a decision to get out of turmoil. I knew right then what I was going to do but honestly had no idea of how I was going to do it.

April 18, 2011

I talked to a lawyer at the courthouse today, had her listen to the recordings, and told her everything that was going on. She had me talk to a domestic violence counselor. That seemed extreme but they said I could file a protection from abuse. I'm terrified to do that because I live with this man! He literally controls all of our money, pays our bills, and the cars are in his name. What if he gets pissed and just takes all of that away and kicks me out or finds another way to destroy me? I keep going back and forth in my head with the best option. I know it's not good to stay with someone just for the kids, but are the kids truly better off without him and me providing for them together?

April 20, 2011

Well, I did it. I filed the damn papers. I'm still so scared. She told me it's not public. He doesn't get served papers at work or anything, and the police don't show up. I asked for a resolution by him going to counseling and taking anger management classes, domestic violence classes, and parenting classes. I feel like that's reasonable and something he should have been doing since I asked him about it before. If he doesn't do those things and the judge agrees, then that's where it becomes a bigger issue. I just hope he does this stuff and things change.

I can't believe I actually had to write this stuff down and he is going to read it. I don't know what he will do when he sees it, but I'm just praying he stays calm and understands why I did it.

- Extreme verbal abuse against me and our child (name-calling, feelings of worthlessness, aggressive yelling, and threatening physical violence)
- Physical abuse against our child (severe spanking, rough arm grabbing, and hair pulling)
- Emotional abuse (threats of suicide, degrading comments, and unpredictable mood swings)

April 23, 2011

Finally, some good news!!! I got accepted into the teaching program. I feel so relieved. I have NO IDEA how this is all going to work. I will be gone in the summer for, like, 7 weeks for the training and then have a new job. It's all so much and so fast, but I really can't wait. Most of the people in the program are coming right out of college, so I'm definitely older than most, but we get to stay in the dorms and study together. I feel like it's a little bit of a second chance at college, except this time I have two kids, and I certainly won't be doing drugs, LOL.

May 1, 2011

Life is crazy. We had our first bout for roller derby, and you can't even guess what happened. So I was the jammer, which means I skate around as fast as possible and the other team tries to catch me. And by catch me, I mean HIT ME! Well, the other team was chasing me down, and one of the blockers went in helmet-first and bashed me right in my collarbone. Immediately, I felt an incredibly warm pain shoot up my arm. I skated to the center of the rink so I didn't get hit again but didn't realize that I made it so the ref couldn't stop the clock. As soon as time was up, I limped off holding my arm and knew something was very wrong. They had to put me in a wheelchair and take me to the hospital. I felt so bad because my whole family was there watching, even Bri and Ashley. Everyone was worried, but I was kind of laughing because it was just so ridiculous. I think they said it's a compound fracture or something, so they want to do surgery so that it heals properly. I reeeeeallly don't want to do surgery, but if it's the only way to fix this, then I don't think I have a choice.

May 15, 2011

I got the surgery and am finally able to write a little bit. I've been hopped up on painkillers. Honestly, I was a little nervous to take them, so I really haven't taken them too much, but the pain was so intense the first few days that I needed them to sleep. They ended up putting a metal bar and two screws in my collarbone. I still can't lift or move my right arm at all. It's been really hard nursing the baby. I had some milk frozen for her to drink while I was on the painkillers, but now I'm pretty much off them, so I'm going to start nursing her again. I have no idea how I can do this with one arm, but I'm certainly going to try. We didn't come all this way for nothing!

May 20, 2011

I've been feeling a bit of depression coming on. I don't know how to describe it, but it's like an overwhelming sadness and a little bit of hopelessness. Almost like a wave washing over me or a sunken feeling that has grown inside of me. I actually feel a bit empty...I'm still recovering from the surgery and can't really do anything for myself. It's been easiest to stay upstairs in bed, but Jason doesn't even come to see me or hang out other than to check on me or bring me the baby when she needs to nurse. I asked him if he could help me shower and brush my hair, and he just said no. He

didn't give me a reason or answer why. He just isn't going to
do it. It just seems cruel if you ask me.

MOM LIFE

June 20, 2011

Ahhh, I can't believe it's almost here. I'm packing for teacher training and leave this weekend! Most people are staying there the whole time, but because it's only an hour away, I'm going to come home on Friday afternoon and then back on Sunday afternoon. This way I can see the kids and drop off all the milk I pump during the week. Thank goodness I've gotten some stocked up, but it's going to be really crazy trying to save it all while I'm there. I'm staying in a dorm with a roommate, and hopefully, she doesn't mind me pumping all the time. Jason doesn't seem to mind that he will be home alone with the kids during the week. I'm a little nervous, but I actually think that without me here, he won't be triggered as much—or at least I hope he isn't. It's not like I have any other choices, and I don't know that skipping this training and staying home is the best answer for the long run. I just pray we all come out okay.

June 27, 2011

Things are just next level here. I can hardly explain how hard and long each day is. We teach the whole first half of the day and then do training for the second half. I've somehow managed to make my schedule work so that I can pump every 3 to 4 hours. It's a bit absurd because I have to hide in a random classroom, and it's blazing hot here. There is NO air conditioner, and I'm always worried I'm missing something. Jackie, one of the other teachers, and I have become super close. We both work at the same school and ride the bus together. We automatically became best friends. It's just nice to have someone else here that I can connect with and talk about all this craziness.

July 2, 2011

I have had no time at all to write. This training is absolutely insane. We are gone all day from 7 AM to 4 PM, then come straight back to the dorms to study and lesson plan. It's even harder for me than everyone else because I'm driving home on the weekends and have a freakin' family to take care of, so I don't get any rest. Not to mention everyone here is bonding and hanging out together, but I'm not there during any of the downtime. It's a little lonely, but I'm still loving it. I can do this. I've done hard things before. At least the weekends at home are pretty peaceful. I'm actually a little shocked. It's giving me some hope. Jason and I aren't seeing each other all week anyway, and once I get back, I really just want to spend all my time with the kids so he gets a break and can do what he wants. Even during the week, we aren't talking much unless it's me calling to video chat with them. I miss the kids so much, and I do feel guilty for missing some of the baby's firsts. She took her first steps when I was home last weekend, though!!! Okay, back to lesson planning. Gotta go!

July 8, 2011

We had the BEST time last night. They had these signs all over the dorm rooms that said, "The Drop at 10." We had no clue what it was. Honestly, I thought they were going to haze us or we were going to have to do push-ups, LOL. We were clueless. Then at 10 o'clock, we all showed up where we were supposed to be, and it was a dance party. The shock and excitement on our faces were priceless. They played all kinds of old-school 90's music and had snacks. It was so silly, but we were HYPE! It was like the first glimmer of fun we had in weeks, and we NEEDED it. None of us wanted to leave when it was over.

August 22, 2011

It's all happening! Last week we interviewed with three different schools and then chose our favorite. I was matched with the school I listed as my first choice. I'll be teaching kindergarten next week. I was able to buy all this old teaching stuff from a teacher who taught kindergarten for the last 30 years. She had so much stuff. I'm doing a whole theme for my classroom, so I've got to decorate and get everything ready. I even brought the girls in with me this week so I could set up and still spend time with them.

August 25, 2011

I feel so conflicted right now. Parts of my life are so good and exciting, but home is just terror. He never went and did any of the things he was supposed to do from the court order a few months ago, and of course, he is blaming me because I went to teacher training, so *how was he supposed to do that when he was "stuck home watching the kids"?* I don't know, but he should have figured it out if he wanted to save this marriage. I honestly think I'm just done. I'm so miserable, and he is miserable too. I've still been keeping the voice memos to make sure I'm hearing the things he says, because sometimes when I think back to these situations, it feels unbelievable. He SCREAMS. Literally screaming at us, and his look of disgust makes me feel like the smallest person in the world. I thought your husband was supposed to be your partner, the person who lifts you up, but he is literally the person who makes me feel the worst about myself. It's like he knows I can't leave, and now that I've changed careers and make literally HALF the income of what I was making before, I don't even know how I could afford to leave. What does that look like? Me and two kids, paying rent, buying food, and paying all the bills. Is that even possible? I feel trapped. I need to leave, but fuck, I'm stuck.

August 28, 2011

One good thing about this new career is it's like another fresh start. I am finally doing something I love!!! I CHOSE this career. It didn't just fall in my lap. It's not convenient. And it's not something I was forced into out of necessity. I built this! It's mine, and even though I'm making less money and working way harder, I feel really fulfilled.

September 10, 2011

I'm still shaking. I don't even know how this happened. We were coming home from dinner, and the kids were asleep in the car. We started arguing about something stupid, and then he started screaming at me. I was driving and asked him to stop because it was making me nervous and he was going to wake the kids up. He was spiraling and just shouting. At one point, I thought he would try and jerk the wheel to make us all run off the side of the road. He started saying that if I left him, he didn't want to "be here" anymore and threatened to jump out of the car while it was moving. I was really scared. When we got home, I made a quick decision, and when he got out of the car first, I stayed in the car in the driveway and just locked the doors. I did not feel safe going into that house with him and definitely didn't want to bring the kids in. This was the switch I knew was coming, and now he was just enraged. He cares too much about what other people think, so he didn't come outside and bang on the windows or plead with us to come in. He just kept calling my phone endlessly, begging me to come inside and saying that he would calm down and stop. I didn't believe him.

I ended up calling my friend, who said I should call the police since he was trying to hurt himself. It took a lot for me to call them. I know he HATES for our business to be out there. Nobody close to us even knows what has been going on, and I was worried that after all of this died down, he would be even more pissed at me. But what were my other options?? They actually came to the house and talked to him. They said he seemed okay now and took back his threats. I told them I didn't feel safe, so they had him call his brother so he could stay with him for the night and the kids and I could go in the house. I barely slept all night. I just kept thinking he was going to come back home and hurt us.

Maybe it sounds crazy, or I watched too many movies, but I thought he might try to kill us. He was mad. I've seen that rage in his eyes, and I know he can fake it for others, but other people don't see what goes on behind closed doors. I'm pretty sure he HATES me, and he would try to hurt me by hurting the kids. He has tried to break me in other ways, but none of those have worked. He knows the one way he could really get to me is through them, and I could never live with myself if he hurt them. I guess in some ways, he made this decision easier, and now I feel less conflicted about what I want to do. I definitely know what I DON'T want to do, and that is to come home to this feeling, this deep pit in my stomach, every night.

September 12, 2011

I dropped the kids off at daycare this morning and was on my way to work when he called me. He was crying, pleading with me to come home and not go to work today. When I tell you he was in shambles, he was literally falling apart. I've NEVER seen him like this. He sounded so desperate, and I was worried he was going to kill himself. After last night and then this phone call, my head was spinning. But on the other hand, I was pissed. I felt like he was doing this on purpose to ruin the one good thing I had going for me right now, and that was this job. I just started a few weeks ago, and I'm a teacher. You can't just call out the same morning and not come to work. What should I do? I called my principal and told him a little about what was going on and that it was an emergency and I had to call off. Thank goodness he was understanding and told me to take care of whatever I needed.

In my head, I knew if I was taking off work, then something needed to happen. I needed a change ASAP. I wasn't just going home to baby him or make him feel better.

After hours and hours of talking and crying and pleading, he actually went and checked himself into the hospital. I was shocked that he agreed to go get help. I don't know that he had another option. I can't be his counselor, and I don't know what to say to someone when they want to die or are thinking of dying. Hell, I barely know how to keep myself out of that dark place. I felt so relieved when I dropped him off. I literally exhaled a huge, deep breath and sobbed in my car. This feels like a turning point. Like something can change now—for the better. I know what it's like there, so I'm sure he isn't going to like it, but maybe it will give him some peace and introspection. Hell, he can't hide it anymore. I don't even know what to tell his family or what to do, but I do feel like the kids and I can get some sleep tonight and know that he is safe and getting what he needs.

September 13, 2011

I went back to work today, and the kids were sooo cute. They said they missed me yesterday and were asking where I was. It was a bit chaotic getting back in the groove and trying to stay focused, but their hugs meant everything!

September 16, 2011

Jason is back home. He only stayed a couple of days and not the full week like they recommended, but he was ready. We talked for a LONG time tonight and are going to try to make this thing work. When he talked, he really sounded different—like he gets it now. He was so apologetic for all

the things that happened and was telling me how depressed
he was and that was making him angry and lash out. He
never wanted to make us feel bad, but he couldn't help it.
I guess he felt safe to express his feelings with us and was
bottling it up everywhere else, so we got the worst of it.
I decided to just wipe the slate clean and really give him
a fresh start. I think if we want this to work, I can't hold
anything over his head or resent him. I have to truly give
him a clean slate and act like we have a new relationship. He
agreed to go to couples counseling and individual counseling,
so I'm hopeful! This is the best-case scenario.

September 20, 2011

Things have been so good! Work is hard. Our kids are
crazy, BUT we are making it work. We have been cooking
dinners together, and Jason is actually playing with the kids.
He still wants everything clean, of course, but he has been
getting on the floor and hanging out with them while they
play. I'm glad to see some good changes.

October 19, 2011

Sooooo, we did NOT plan this, but guess who is pregnant
again?!?! I can hardly believe it. I'm shocked, to be honest.
A mom of THREE?? I was feeling pretty tired and missed my
period this month. I didn't even think anything of it because

we had so much trouble conceiving last time and my cycle is always off. My periods are always sporadic, so I never know if my period is late or what is going on. I don't know what told me to take a test, but I just had a feeling. Of course, I'm a bit nervous because we are still working on this marriage stuff, but I'm glad it happened, and maybe it will keep us going in this positive direction.

November 5, 2011

That didn't last long at all. I can't believe it's all happening again. We were in the honeymoon phase for a few weeks, and now I feel like it's back to the same thing again. He is always stressed. I'm stressed, and now I'm freaking pregnant. I feel crazy at this point. What am I supposed to do? He knows I'm trapped now. I don't know what I was expecting, but he really gave me hope. I really thought this time was different, and we're married. This isn't like the boyfriends before. We are supposed to stay together, and now we have 2 kids; plus, he adopted Brianna. Why did I let him do that? I feel like the worst mother possible. He adopted Brianna so I could protect her from Floyd, and now he is just as bad, if not worse. It pisses me off even more that nobody else even knows what is going on. He fakes it so well in front of everyone. Every time we hang out with our friends, he just acts like this happy, nice guy. And then, of course, I'm trying to pick little fights so he will freak out in front of them, and he just looks at me strangely, and I look like the crazy one. He turns it around so I'm the one who gets frustrated and annoyed, then I just look like the nagging, annoying wife, and he is the cool, calm, collected husband. It is INFURIATING!!! I can't take it much longer.

November 29, 2011

I've just had enough. I keep trying, keep going back to him and forgiving him, and he keeps blaming me for everything. I don't think I'm a bad person. I'm not a bad mom. All he does is put me down, and the kicker is that he is getting louder and angrier and more violent. He hasn't hit me yet, but I feel it coming. After that whole car incident and now that I've stayed AND I'm pregnant, he knows I'm vulnerable. This is what happened with the last asshole. It's like they know you're weaker when you're pregnant, so they push more buttons or get more violent, knowing it can hurt you and the baby, and you can't really do anything about it. Imagine wanting to make someone fearful of you. Why? I don't get it. I'm not even sure I'm actually in love with him or even love him. But here I am... Where the hell would I even go? How would I even go anywhere? There isn't extra money lying around, and I can't just quickly run away. I've been trying to think up plans for how this could all happen, and I'm lost. I would need a deposit for rent and to find a place that is close to the kids' daycare.

December 1, 2011

    I want to tell my friends what's happening, but I'm scared. What if I tell them all this shit and then we stay together? Or what if I tell them and they don't believe me? They never see this side of him. My parents don't even know. I tried to talk to his mom before, but she is living in la-la land. It's like she doesn't know her son at all. To be honest, I think she is faking her marriage, too. When we were living with them before, they would fight all the time behind closed doors and then act like nothing happened. It's this whole fake white picket fence crap. I should have known then. I should have seen the signs, but I didn't. I thought he just wasn't close to his siblings because everyone was busy or they were younger, but now I get it. It's all just fake. They all just pretend. I'm sick of pretending. I feel like I'm screaming on the inside. I want to rip my skin off and get out!

FREEDOM

January 1, 2012

New year of bullshit. If I hear one more person say, "New year, new me," I'm going to punch them in the throat. It's a new year, and I'm the same damn me I've always been. Spent the night with my pregnant self and the kids. I couldn't bear to be around him or our friends anymore. Can I even call them all friends if I'm not willing to trust them with this secret? He just makes me look psychotic in front of them, and they are none the wiser—eating up his lame jokes, which are usually pointed towards me. I couldn't stand it anymore and went home last night.

I will say, the kids and I had so much fun blowing party horns and banging pots and pans together. Plus, I'm pregnant. It's not like I could even drink to escape the reality of this nonsense. Hopefully, his hungover ass stays in bed for a while.

January 11, 2012

I went to the courthouse today and filed for emergency protection from abuse. He hasn't made any steps toward what he was supposed to do in the original order, and it expires in a few months. We had a hearing right away, and I asked for no contact. I wrote down quotes of all the stuff he said in my recordings and discussed his anger, trying to jump out of the car, and threatening to hurt himself as a way to keep us around. I got to see the judge right away, and because he didn't do any of actions he was supposed to do from the last order, she gave him 6 months of no contact—no phone calls, no visits, nothing. I don't even know how I feel right now. She listened to the recordings I had on my phone and was disgusted. She said I was really brave to do this and that most women don't come forward. That made me feel so good because I've been conflicted and feeling like he wasn't abusing us enough to take these steps. It's still hard to think of it as abuse.

Of course I am still worried about him because the baby is due in June, so he may not even be able to be there for the birth since he can't be around us for six months. She gave me time to find a place to live and said I could stay in the house with the kids, and he would need to stay somewhere else until I found a place. I took all of the money in our savings and transferred it to myself for now so that he couldn't wipe it clean—which I KNOW he would do the second he found out about this. I'm afraid to go home or even call him right now. I guess I can't even call him. Good thing he isn't supposed to call me either. My whole body is shaking, but I'm just taking the next step like Erin said. One foot in front of the other. I need to calm down and figure out what's next.

I called my dad and told him a little about what was going on and that I needed to move out. He didn't ask too many questions but said he would look for apartments right away.

January 21, 2012

He is staying with his brother again. My dad found this cute little townhouse. It's closer to my work, and my grandmother said she could come watch Ashley at my house during the day so that I could save money on daycare and Bri could take the bus down the street. I'm actually surprised that this is all working out pretty smoothly.

February 2, 2012

I can't believe I'm doing this. Yesterday was move-in day. I'm fucking pregnant and now a single mom of three. Who does this? Apparently, I do. I'm scared shitless, but somehow I just know I can do this on my own and will be happier doing it. I've been doing it already anyway. He seems to think we are just separated like when I moved into the hotel for a week. It's different this time, though. You don't move out of your "happy" home in the suburbs and sign a lease if you think you're coming back. He must have hope. I guess he thought he had me twisted around his finger a little bit tighter than I actually was. Well, now with the PFA (Protection From Abuse) order, I don't have to hear his screaming or be worried about him putting his hands on any of us. You should have seen his face when I showed up in the courtroom with a transcription of all the voice recordings I had taken over the last several months. The things he said were so disgusting that even the judge didn't want to read them out loud. He consented to everything and said he would do counseling and parent classes. Well, that shit is not enough. You were supposed to do all of that last time.

THE INFAMOUS U-HAUL

February 14, 2012

I've had to get all new furniture and unpack all of these boxes. Honestly, it's nice having my own space and choosing how I want it to be—nobody giving their opinion or telling me where things have to go. I'm exhausted and overwhelmed sometimes, but one thing I don't have to worry about is the terror of someone constantly bashing me or the kids over and over. Bri asked what happened to daddy, and I just told her he has to work on some things so he can be a better daddy and that we'll stay here for a while. She didn't really ask any questions after that and seemed satisfied with the answer. She definitely seems happier and lighter. She doesn't jump anymore when she makes a mess or spills anything, and I've seen her being silly and giggling more. This is why I did this. They deserve to be happy.

March 1, 2012

Things are a bit wild. My grandmother has been helping with the kids. She helps get Bri on the bus in the mornings then watches Ashley all day at my house. It's been really helpful but still intrusive in a way. Then my dad comes over whenever he wants without calling and starts fixing things or hanging pictures. I'm not trying to be a brat, but I need some privacy, my own space without everyone's opinions. I know they are all just trying to take care of me in their own way, but I just kinda want to figure it out on my own.

March 5, 2012

I know I shouldn't do this, but I feel guilty. I took him from his kids! I've been letting him send videos and audio to the kids. I even created a private YouTube channel and posted videos of them there so he doesn't miss major milestones. I just feel like it's the right thing to do.

Would you believe he had the audacity to write me an email talking about how he shut the girls' bedroom doors and acted like he was in the military on leave away from his family? That's what you're pretending now? You're acting like you did some honorable thing, and THAT'S why you can't see your kids??? Idiot. You hurt us. That's why you can't see us.

March 22, 2012

My feelings are a bit hurt that most of our friends didn't even reach out to see what the hell happened. I basically just disappeared and moved out. What story is he telling them? What do they think? I get the husbands wouldn't reach out, but what about all the women, the wives? These people were my FRIENDS—or at least I thought they were. I can see how maybe they're hurt. I didn't tell them or give them all the details, but if I had told them what was going on, they would have told their husbands, who would have told my husband, which would have been a mess. I just thought somebody would have called to check in on me at this point.

THE GIGGLES ARE THE BEST PART

May 14, 2012

I'm trying to enjoy all of these moments. The good and the bad. The girls are loving this place. We have the cutest little backyard with a sprinkler. I love watching them play and making dinners. This pregnancy is tough, and I'm tired a lot. I have to lesson plan after they both go to bed and then get up early in the morning, but I'm doing it. Jason surprisingly started doing the parenting classes, so I'm thinking of letting him come visit the kids for an hour or two some days while I'm home. This baby is going to come any day now, and I don't want him to miss it. I think it's something I would always regret.

June 13, 2012

I need to go into labor ASAP! It was the last day of school, and we were sitting in meetings all day for professional development. I thought I peed myself, but no...I'm leaking amniotic fluid, and I have 24 hours before I have to deliver or get a C-section. Here we go.

June 17, 2012

Welp! Needless to say, I got myself into labor! Castor oil and lots of walking. I did let Jason come to the birth, and my mom was there, too. Since I actually made it to the birth center this time, I was able to go home a few hours after I delivered. Now I have THREE GIRLS!!! I can't believe it. I let him stay the last couple of nights, which was really helpful. We both slept on the couch with the baby, and he was able to help me a little bit. It was nice just to have someone there to get things for the other girls too. We are all so in love. She is just the sweetest little thing. <3

SELF-LOVE

August 12, 2012

Sorry it's been so long. As you can imagine, things have been busy with the little one. It's been marvelous having the whole summer off and getting to spend time with the girls. I feel like it's been a great way to rest and recover and repair our relationship. Not with Jason, LOL, but with the girls. I feel like I can be really present for them right now, when before, I just felt scattered and confused. Single mom life is not freaking easy, but I am lucky we have figured out the finance stuff so that it works for both of us. It's like I'm getting an "allowance," but I'll take it for now. I was able to file the real divorce papers now that we have officially been separated for over 6 months. I don't think he thought I was going to do it. I actually think he thought I was going to move back in once the baby came. No, sir! I MOVED OUT!!! That was the last straw.

This is exactly where I'm supposed to be.

September 12, 2012

We live right by the cutest little park. The kids and I love going over there. The other day we had a picnic and brought snacks. They went to the playground while I stayed with the baby. The sun was shining and the birds were chirping. It was like a movie scene. I looked around for a moment and was able to just breathe. I've never felt peace like this. It's hard to explain because some days are freakin' hard— like REALLY hard—but then in these little moments, I'm just so grateful for all that has happened.

CHECK OUT THOSE SMILES!

October 17, 2012

Jason has been getting supervised visits with the girls. It's been a nice transition for me. I feel like the kids are safe since one of my family members has to be there, and it gives me a break to go do things for myself. It's usually only a couple of hours at a time at my house, but it's better than nothing. The other day I actually went to get a massage. It was the most glorious time ever. A full hour of rest and relaxation without having this massive responsibility. I need to do more things like this. I've been trying to get in some gym time before picking up all the kids after work, but it's a struggle. Luckily I get out around 4 PM and they are all able to stay in daycare until 6 PM. Of course, I never want to keep them there that late, but I can usually run in and out of the gym by 5 PM and get to them shortly after. Next is a mad dash to get dinner cooked and ready, a sprinkle of playtime, then bath and bed. I keep thinking things will slow down a bit, but the week is just crazy. There is no time to think or even sulk about my situation, but I keep reminding myself this is still better than what I was experiencing before. I just want to be the happy, present mom for my kids, and I'm working towards that every day. I know I did the right thing to start breaking these cycles of abuse. I watched my mom go through it, and I'm sure my grandmother went through it, too. I wouldn't be able to sleep at night if I watched my girls grow up and have the same kind of relationships that all the women in our family have experienced. At least for now, I can sleep well knowing I made a tough but necessary choice.

December 19, 2012

My mom actually surprised me with the best Christmas present ever. I thought we were all just going to Washington, D.C., as a trip for my grandmother. We were all hanging out in this museum when I turned around and saw the officer who used to hang outside of Calvin's apartment. The same

ME AND OFFICER SECKLER REUNITED

officer who quite literally held my hand while I was pregnant and helped me resolve all the issues with my car and warrants for my arrest. I just about lost it. I'm not usually a hugger, but I grabbed this man so tight and sobbed. It's not often you get these full-circle moments where you can thank someone for truly caring about you. I felt so proud to show him that his kindness did not go unnoticed and that I took that extra help and ran with it. I didn't go back to the streets. I didn't fall into another trap. I have 3 amazing girls that I'm raising with confidence. I have a solid career (helping others!), and I'm actually living my life now. I really hope I made him proud. I think he even had a little tear in his eye, too. This is one of those moments you just can't explain in words. You truly had to be there. I dream of telling this story to the girls one day so that they can understand how just one person, one moment, can change a life.

January 17, 2013

Jackie and I went out to a dive bar tonight. I don't even know what brought us there. It's in the college town, and we were clearly out of place. What's more strange is that college kids weren't even in the bar. It was an older crowd filled with guys clinking their beer glasses and beating their chests to show who was more manly. We walked in with our tight pleather pants and sparkly tops, and you could just hear the music come to a screeching halt and everyone's heads turn.

Once we got past the door, there was a registration table for a radio show. They were giving away an all-expenses-paid trip to see the Phillies at spring training in Clearwater, Florida. There was no catch, and we just had to put our name and contact info on the list to be entered. We carried on with our night and thought nothing of it. In the back of my head, I just KNEW we were winning this trip. Would you believe that at the end of the night, they called my name?!?! We are going to Florida, baby!! I have no clue who is gonna watch the kids and how I'm getting a week off work from teaching, but I've gotta make this happen. This is a once-in-a-lifetime trip and something I need for my soul! Cross your fingers that I can figure out the details.

February 2, 2013

It's final!!! Your girl is single and ready to mingle. Okay, we probably aren't mingling just yet, but I'm definitely ready to date and just meet people. I feel like my whole life I've never "dated" people. We usually meet and immediately become boyfriend and girlfriend. I want to actually take time to get to know someone, get to know several people. I am really interested in finding out what qualities I like, what I need, and who actually compliments me. I don't even know what I'm looking for at this point. Jason and I made a pact to talk with each other and let each other meet whoever we are dating before introducing them to the kids. That is a long way away, but I'm glad we can be civil. Now that we are separated—well, divorced—things have been so much easier. We both have been learning how to co-parent and communicate, and I like that I'm beginning to trust him. We were both able to come to an agreement on the custody stuff, and he actually finished the parenting class, so I feel much better about him being alone with the kids now. I just pray he has actually made some big changes. The part I never really considered is now that we are divorced and don't live together, if he does lash out or continue his abusive behaviors, there is literally nobody there to protect the kids anymore. It feels strange that I have to send them to his house after all that's happened, and I just have to pretend or hope he has "cured" himself.

February 5, 2013

It's all happening. My boss made an exception to let me take off this whole week and go on the trip to Florida. Normally this would be impossible, but I literally begged him. Jackie and I have been heading to the gym almost every day after work. We are so motivated, and I feel so good. I haven't been away from the kids for more than maybe 24 hours at a time, so that is going to be tough. Honestly, it's been almost 10 years since I've been alone or had time to myself, and I'm really excited to see what that is like. No diapers to change, nobody to worry about getting to bed. I don't have to get anyone dressed or make sure they cross the street safely. I'm either going to crawl into the hotel bed and sleep for a week or go buck wild.

March 18, 2013

In my Meek Mill voice...*HOLD UP WAIT A MINUTE...Y'ALL THOUGHT I WAS FINISHED?* I could get hype off that song no matter what is going on!

I've finally had a few days to decompress and take in everything that happened on that trip. It was everything I ever needed from start to finish. There were ten other people who also won the trip, and we all traveled together. Everyone met at the radio station, and got to know each other. Then our flights were delayed, so we all started going a little delusional in the airport. Everyone was filled with excitement, and we just wanted to get to Clearwater ASAP! All expenses paid: the hotel, flights, and the food. They even had events planned for us to see the brewery, go to one of the spring training games, and do nighttime outings. We spent the days lounging on the beach or hanging in the hot tub. I even wore the new blue bikini that I bought. I haven't felt this confident in a while. For a few days, I felt like I could pretend I wasn't a mom. I know that sounds bad, but I don't mean it that way. I just got to have a break and be a PERSON—an INDIVIDUAL. Nobody there even talked about kids. Nobody assumed I even had kids. One night after

CLEARWATER WILL NEVER BE FORGOTTEN!

dancing our asses off, we hitched a ride home in the back of a pickup truck with two of the guys who traveled on the trip with us. I wouldn't have done it if it were just Jackie and me, but the guys were cool and made me feel a bit safer. When will I ever get to ride in the back of a pickup truck with my hair blowing in the wind, screaming out lyrics to songs again? Probably never. For whatever reason, we got back to the room and started jumping on the beds like we were 10 years old. I haven't laughed that hard in a long time. These are the memories I want to have etched in my brain, especially on hard days, days I want to give up or throw in the towel. I may not get these moments often as a mom, but I will definitely cherish them. The best part was coming home to the kids and giving them huge hugs. They all missed me so much, and I couldn't wait to give them all of my attention.

29 YEARS OLD

May 30, 2013

It's my 29th birthday!!! Jeez, ten years ago I didn't think I would make it to 20. I went from listening to harsh, depressing music that talked about killing yourself to blasting Kirk Franklin's "I Smile" while dancing with my kids in the kitchen. Back then I was begging for someone to love me, hoping they would choose me. Now I wake up to three of the sweetest little faces who remind me every day that I'm already chosen. I used to yearn, beg, and plead for the ability to break free—not realizing that freedom lived within me all along.

I still feel so young and have so much of my life ahead of me. I look back at my 19-year-old self and don't even recognize that girl. I will forever be grateful to Brianna for leading me out of the gutter, quite literally, and forcing me into motherhood at an early age. Most would have seen that as a death sentence, but it's truly what brought me back to life—back to my true self. If it weren't for her, I would have been dead long ago. Once I became a mom, I began to live my whole life for my kids. There were no more options to back out or give up. I thank God for that. Some people say you shouldn't lose yourself in motherhood, but what if you were already lost? They tell moms how they have to have their own identity, but what about when you have no clue who you are? What if you didn't give a shit about yourself? What about when your life feels worthless? The kids kept me focused and busy taking care of somebody other than myself, and I needed that. I needed that more than anyone could ever know. I still wonder if I will always look for something to fill a void inside of me. It all started with hurting myself so that I could actually feel the pain, then the drugs to escape it all. I filled myself with donuts and food while I was pregnant just to have a little bit of joy and sought out men's attention so I could pretend I was loved. I think ultimately, becoming a mom healed a part of me. The child who never felt cared for, the teenager who was forgotten, and the adult who was begging to be loved. It's only now I feel like I'm finally starting to live for myself. Of course, I feel guilty doing things for myself and spending time away from them, but I NEED it. They are safe. I've given them the tools and support to live a life that was different from mine. Even on days it's exhausting, I'm still glad they need me, and I'm even more grateful I have the ability to give them the love they need. It keeps me happy and healthy so that I can be an even better mom for them. I'm still not sure that if it were just me, I would take good care of myself. I'm working on the self-worth part. Hell, maybe I'll always have to work on it, but at least for now, things don't feel desperate. I don't feel trapped anymore. I've finally got my spark back. Imagine if I had ended all of this before it even got started. It's hard to look back now and think I didn't want to be here, didn't want to live this life. I have a purpose and reason to be here. Nobody is controlling me or making me feel like shit just for being myself. Heck, I think the kids even like the quirky and silly side of me.

If I ever get to that sunken place again, I'm going to come back and read this. This is my reminder that things do get better. I'm not broken and never too far gone. The world, my world, my kids still need my light—even if it feels dim. Nobody is gonna stop my shine.

ACKNOWLEDGMENTS

Writing this book was the last step in a long process of healing years of unspoken trauma. I've come to find that trauma is not what happens to us, but how we deal with what happens to us. That is what determines the outcome of our minds, bodies, and souls. The words on each of these pages are more than a memory; they are a proclamation, a confirmation that we all can heal, regardless of our circumstances, and I certainly couldn't have done it alone.

To each of my parents: Our story is complicated, but it is ours. I may not have always understood your ways, but I accept the things that have happened and know they have shaped and molded me into the woman I'm proud of today, and for that, I am grateful.

To my husband, my ride or die, my safe place: Thank you for standing beside me through every season and showing me the true meaning of unconditional love. Your unwavering belief in me has helped me believe in myself, even in my darkest moments. The way you accept every part of me makes me feel truly seen. This chaotic life, our love, and this book—I'm endlessly grateful to share them with you. Thank you for being my greatest encourager, my fiercest protector, and my best friend. I love you, always.

To my children, Alexis, Cailin, Haley, and Kaia: You are my

greatest gifts, my deepest joy, and my most profound lessons in love. Being your mother is my life's greatest honor. Each of you has taught me more than you will ever know, and for that, I feel truly blessed. May you always know how deeply you are loved, how limitless your potential is, and how proud I am to be your mom.

To my friends who reminded me my voice matters and should be heard: Thank you. Your belief in me carried me through many moments of doubt.

To those who have been part of my healing journey—mentors, coaches, therapists, yoga teachers, shamans and the ones who saw my heart even when I tried to hide it—this book is, in part, because of you. Thank you for pushing me to grow, asking the hard questions, and reminding me that I am more than my past.

To my readers: If you've ever felt unseen, unheard, or misunderstood, I hope this book brings you clarity—that none of us has it all figured out, comfort in knowing you aren't alone, and the courage to share your own story out loud.

And finally, to my 13-year-old self: Everything is going to be okay. Heck, it's going to be better than okay. You are stronger than you could ever imagine and have so much love and wisdom to share. Don't give up. Your life is worth living, and the people in your life need you to break these cycles. Spoiler alert: the freedom you are looking for? It's on the other side of loving yourself. Pour every ounce of energy into discovering who you are and loving every single part of yourself because the world needs you.

ABOUT THE AUTHOR

A Delaware native, Kristin's journey is deeply woven into the fabric of Wilmington, where she grew up surrounded by the vibrant energy of her community. A storyteller at heart, she has always been drawn to narratives of resilience, transformation, and empowerment—both in her own life and in the lives of those she touches through her work.

Kristin's passion for storytelling first took shape through her dedication to education. She began her career mentoring students at EastSide Charter School, a role that led her to join Teach for America and earn a Master's in Teaching. As a Special Education teacher, she not only fostered academic growth but also championed the importance of self-care, personal development, and the power of one's own voice. Her time coaching a girls' boxing club and stepping into the unexpected role of a basketball coach further fueled her belief that every individual holds an untapped strength waiting to be unlocked.

Her own journey of resilience took a pivotal turn following a traumatic concussion in 2018. This life-altering moment became the catalyst for her entrepreneurial path, leading to the creation of the "Nude Food" healthy food truck, which later evolved into V-Trap Kitchen and Lounge—a wellness-focused eatery in Wilmington. Kristin's ability to pivot and reinvent herself became even more evident during the pandemic when she transitioned into online health coaching and deepened her role in the Launcher entrepreneurship program, helping other entrepreneurs turn their visions into reality.

Amidst all these endeavors, Kristin found a new passion in writing, which helped her heal and process her past trauma. Writing became an outlet of expression and acceptance. In 2024, she became a 2x published author in the collaborative book *Unveiling the Secrets*, where she shared her darkest moments to connect with others and inspire hope. And again in *Unveiling the Secrets: Finally Taking Up Space*, offering a raw, honest, and transformative look at overcoming adversity through honest self-reflection. The words in the following pages exist as a testament to the past. Each diary entry reveals a life full of addiction, pain, and secrets so shameful that she has not shared them until now. None of this reflects the life she leads today—a life built through years of healing, growth, and intentional work. Kristin's writing is meant to evoke emotion and inspire action for readers to take control of their lives and determine their own destinies regardless of the circumstances they are given. Connect with Kristin online as she shares her life and all the ups and downs: www.legendarymindandbody.com.

www.ingramcontent.com/pod-product-compliance
Lightning Source LLC
Chambersburg PA
CBHW020816130626
46554CB00006B/2466